William J. Keimig & Petroc Willey

SERIES EDITORS

Infant Baptism Preparation

A Field Manual

This field manual was authored and edited by a team of catechists, and catechetical leaders led by Jaqueline & Michael Van Hemert.

Steubenville, OH

Art Credits:

Adobe stock digital illustrations by Faith Stock:

Jesus is baptized by John the Baptist in the Jordan River.

The Divine Dove. A radiant dove symbolizing the Holy Spirit in flight over sacred waters.

Radiant Jesus Walking on Water in Vibrant Colors.

Jesus preaching in Galilee and gathering his disciples. Life of Jesus.

The birth of Moses — Exodus 2.

Painting of Jesus walking on water. Silhouette under the moonlight.

The moment symbolizing the disciples' mission to make disciples of all nations.

Copyright © 2025 by Franciscan University of Steubenville

All rights reserved. This book or any portion thereof may not be reproduced or used in any manner whatsoever without the express written permission of the publisher except for the use of brief quotations in a book review.

The Catechetical Institute at
Franciscan University of Steubenville,
114 Brady Circle East, Steubenville, OH 43952

https://FranciscanAtHome.com

Print ISBN: 978-0-9893576-2-3

Acknowledgments:

We want to offer our profound thanks to Jacqueline and Michael van Hemert, experienced, faithful and creative catechetical practitioners in the home and the parish, the main authors of this text, together with all of the wonderful collaborators who have made this field manual possible through the generous sharing of their perspectives from the field of ministry together with their theological and catechetical wisdom: Martha Drennan, Dino Durando, Laura Gallant, Carol Harnett, Jill Kerekes, Dane Kirk, Sr Hyacinthe Defos du Rau, O.P., Joann Roa, Tim Seman, Lori Smith, Joseph White, and Margaret Wickware. Within the Franciscan Catechetical Institute team, we would also especially like to thank Marie Higgins, Madison McCalister and Daniel Rivera.

Petroc Willey and William J Keimig

Parrhesia:

Straightforward simplicity, filial trust, joyous assurance, humble boldness, the certainty of being loved (CCC 2778)

Table of Contents

9 — Introduction
Getting Your Feet Wet

25 — Step 1: Your Dream
A Vision for this Ministry

43 — Step 2: God's Dream
Come to the Waters

63 — Step 3: The Rite Stuff
Church Teaching

77 — Step 4: The Upstream Opportunity
Principles for Recalibration

99 — Step 5: Program Planning
Master Planning Worksheet

Step 6: Choose Your Own Adventure

138	The Good News: *How to Keep Catechesis Kerygmatic*
146	The Team: *Finding and Forming Catechists*
156	The Need: *Skills for Building Lasting Relationships with Families*
166	The Co-Laborers: *Working with Godparents*
172	The Parent's Meeting: *The Unique Needs of Mothers and Fathers*
180	The Holy Family: *Helping Families of Young Children enter into Deeper Prayer*
186	The Window of Opportunity: *Ministering to Families with Children under Six*
192	The Village: *Involving Your Parish Community in Baptism Preparation*
196	The Exceptions to the Rule: *Ministering in Special Situations*

Helpful Tools, Programs, and Resources	220
Bibliography	230
Endnotes	236
Who We Are	246

Introduction

Getting Your Feet Wet

"... Go therefore and make disciples of all nations, baptizing them in the name of the Father and of the Son and of the Holy Spirit..." [1]

∼

I F YOU'RE READING THIS LITTLE BOOK, IT PROBABLY MEANS that you've somehow — by virtue of volunteering or being volunteered — found yourself in charge of an infant Baptism preparation program. Perhaps you're a priest, a deacon, a parish catechetical leader, or a faithful member of your parish who said "yes" to serving in this ministry at the request of a persuasive pastor. It's possible that you have a team of people ready to help you, but it's just as possible that you're going it alone. If you're paid, it may not be that much. If you're volunteering, you're likely squeezing it in between a full-time job or full-time family responsibilities. Maybe you have a wealth of resources and a generous budget, or perhaps, you're pinching pennies and counting parish paper clips to save a few cents. You might belong to a 30-family parish in the countryside, a 15,000-family congregation in a large city, or something in between. Regardless of where you're coming from or what your parish circumstances look like, there's still one thing that you have in common with everyone else, who also picked up a copy of this book.

God has called *you*.

Here.

And now.

To this ministry.

For such a time as this.

God has invited *you* to wade into the waters of infant baptismal preparation, not only for the sake of those who will be cleansed by its waters, but also for your own sake. (As we, and a great many others who have come before us, like to say: "The soul that the Lord is most concerned about saving is always your own." [2]) So, let us congratulate you on saying "yes" to this beautiful work that is certainly not without its challenges, but very ripe with literal new beginnings.

Whether you're a seasoned ministry veteran who's done baptismal preparation ministry a million times before, or this is your very first time taking the plunge, think of this book as a helpful guide, walking with *you*, accompanying *you*, and enabling *you*, the leader, to navigate your unique and particular circumstances with wisdom, strength, creativity, and faithfulness. After all, who among us hasn't browsed through a magisterial document like Saint John Paul II's *Catechesi tradendae* only to find ourselves overwhelmed by the heightened language, confused about how to practically implement it into a shared parish with part-time staff, or discouraged at the state of our own ministry compared to the sweeping vision of what catechesis is supposed to look like?

Dear friend, fear not! What Mother Church gives us is good, true, beautiful, and incredibly useful, but it was not meant for us to digest all by ourselves. Saint Augustine mentored and encouraged Deogratias,[3] when he was struggling with the state of his own ministry, and Augustine returns over and over again to the problem of weary and apathetic listeners! In the same way, this book aims to mentor and encourage you, while you're figuring out the best way forward. Thus, this book is not a textbook. It's not a slick series of tips and tricks to tell you how to do your job better. And it's not a brand-new

Baptism prep curriculum guaranteed to transform your program and plug that post-baptismal leak overnight, as great as that would be!

Instead, consider this book to be a field manual, written to those who are serving "in the trenches" of parish ministry. Although you might not need to dig a literal trench or navigate actual boobytraps, you will need to dig out that Order of Baptism book from the sacristy and navigate the actual world of parents who haven't been to Mass since they were confirmed, yet are committed to baptizing their baby in the Catholic Church. Whether you're a lone soldier, a small platoon, or a modest army trying to find your way through ministerial minefields, this little book just might become your go-to handbook.

> ## Field Manual [definition]
>
> From the Cambridge Dictionary.
>
> *[noun] "A book giving information to soldiers about their work."*
>
> Like any good field manual, this book will offer you a succinct "Commander's Intent" for your ministerial work — the universal principles and proper protocol given to us by Mother Church for the battlefield. Because we must never forget that we're not just punching a clock (even if you're doing this for free), we are pushing back the darkness, by bringing the Light, Jesus.[4] It cannot be underestimated, nor can we lose sight, that we are in a spiritual war for human souls and their eternal destination. C.S. Lewis described that world as "Enemy-occupied territory." He wrote, "Christianity is the story of how the rightful king has landed, you might say landed in disguise, and is calling us all to take part in a great campaign of sabotage." [5] We are bringing Good News of freedom in Christ.

> We're not ones to cry "spiritual warfare" every time something gets a bit difficult, but it's worth remembering that there *really* are evil forces at work, and they *really* don't like the goal that the Holy Spirit is trying to accomplish through the ministry of the Church ... and through you: the goal of souls living now and for eternity in the Life and Love of the Trinity — Father, Son, and Holy Spirit.

On the other side of these pages are real people who have been (and still are) elbows deep in real ministry. We are familiar with the highs and the lows, the challenges and the opportunities, the joys and the sorrows. We also know that those in leadership are often left behind (ever heard the saying "it's lonely at the top?") and more liable to the snares of pride, burnout, and isolation. Therefore, we believe it is critical to form those who form others, giving leaders the support, encouragement, and guidance they need to help them stay close to Jesus, to follow the Church faithfully, and to be effective and on-fire catechists. If it were up to us, we'd be sitting at a table together with a warm beverage and fresh-baked pastries. We would pray and strategize, taking the universal principles given to us by Mother Church and creatively adapting them to *your* parish's infant baptismal preparation process. Since we haven't figured out a way to teleport ourselves to you quite yet, we humbly give you the next best thing: this little book. Even if just on paper or a screen, we really are *with* you. We are *for* you. And you don't need to do this alone. Be assured of the prayers of Franciscan University and its *Catechetical Institute*.

The Perfect Pairing

Like peanut butter needs jelly and tortilla chips beg for good salsa, this book is designed to pair with the 2020 *Directory for Catechesis*. The *Directory for Catechesis* was released by the Pontifical Council for the Promotion of the New Evangelization, and is a how-to-guide for those of us practicing catechesis *in our own time*. That's the key phrase. After all, how else are we to navigate the tension of a Gospel that stays the same forever and a culture that very much does not? The Church has been entrusted to guard the Deposit of Faith — Sacred Scripture and Sacred Tradition with the Magisterium's authoritative interpretation and to present this Deposit faithfully through the "literary forms of modern thought." [6]

This particular *Directory* is the third in a series (first was the *General Catechetical Directory* released in 1971 and the second was the *General Directory for Catechesis* released in 1997), each written to frame catechesis with fundamental *principles*, often after the publication of important magisterial documents, such as the *Catechism of the Catholic Church (Catechism* or CCC) in 1992. The 2020 *Directory* gives us marching orders for effectively reaching a culture deeply changed by digitization and globalization. Highlights of the *Directory* include:

- The identity, vocation, and formation of catechists

- Heavy emphasis on the *kerygma* and what that looks like

- The need for all catechesis to be inspired by the catechumenal model (OCIA or Order of Christian Initiation of Adults)

- A closer look at the relationship between catechesis and evangelization

- Challenges for catechists to avoid a "one-size-fits-all" batching approach

- A call for catechists to accompany each individual in his or her unique response of faith.

A Crash Course in the OCIA

A resounding theme in the *Directory* is the catechumenate — the OCIA — as the source of inspiration for *all* catechesis. And that means our infant Baptism approach, as well.

Of course, unless you're also in charge of the OCIA yourself, you may not be familiar with what that means. The catechumenate is the ancient, early-Church practice for initiating the unbaptized into Christian faith and life. It went into the background around the fourth century, because Christianity had spread so far and wide that there was no need for the same kind of intense missionary activity there had been in the first few centuries of the Church. The Second Vatican Council restored it and we can understand why, because we can see in our lives that the missionary nature of catechesis has "become weakened over time." [7]

In summary, the catechumenate is a **process**, taking place in four **stages**, punctuated by **liturgical rites**, all designed to gradually lead the catechumen (the unbaptized person) into full encounter with "the mystery of Christ in the life of the community." [8] It is the "*typical setting* of initiation, catechesis, and mystagogy," [9] a "model for all catechesis." [10] In other words, if we want our catechesis to bear fruit and spark conversion in the families we minister to, then we should look to the OCIA as our framework.

As leaders in infant baptismal preparation, we cannot copy the catechumenate strictly, but we should have a thorough understanding of the catechumenal process's four stages, such that it inspires our preparation and gives us the vision to see these stages in the learners, in order to meet them where they are at. Two excellent resources for growing in your understanding of the OCIA can be found on the Catechetical Institute's website, Franciscan at Home; we recommend the workshops "The Catechumenal Process: A Modern Restoration of an Ancient Practice," and "The Catechumenate: Paradigm for all Catechesis."

❈ Task: Good Soil ❈

Let's pause here, just for a minute.

Throughout this book, toward the end of each chapter, you'll find several "pauses" designed to help you work through or "workshop" the content from each chapter. It may be tempting to skip these "pauses" and hurry back to the grind of all the work that is incessantly calling your name. We challenge you otherwise and even proffer that the Holy Spirit has much for you in these pauses. To miss these pauses would be to miss the real "work" of a ministry that bears deep and lasting spiritual fruit. Listen. There is another voice calling your name.

For just a few minutes, set aside your laptop or your notebook. Turn your phone to silent. Find a quiet and peaceful sacred space where you can be alone with Jesus. Really, go do it now. Bring this book along.

Now, breathe in. Breathe out slowly. Close your eyes, if you like. Hear your Savior speak your name. Think of Him smiling at you. Feel the warmth of His Presence. Remember that before you are a priest, a deacon, or a parish catechetical leader, you are first His child. The Lord "delights in you." [11]

Once your own spirit has quieted, invite the Holy Spirit to "overshadow you," as He did Mary, the mother of Jesus.[12] In preparing families for the Sacrament of Baptism, catechesis is not unlike the seed in the parable of the sower.[13] It can fall onto the path; it can be blown away; it can land among the thorns; it can wedge itself into the rocky ground . . . or it can be received into rich soil. If we desire this area of ministry to be fruitful, we must first prepare the "soil" of our own hearts.

For this task, we're going to read the parable of the sower from the Gospel of Matthew 13:1–23. Go ahead now and read through this passage at a moderate pace.

Next, read it a second time, a little slower and out loud, making note of any words or phrases that catch your eye or your heart. What in this passage stands out to you? What in this passage challenges you? What in this passage comforts you?

Finally, read the passage a third time, then reflect. In the field of our own hearts, we have areas of rich soil, and we also have patches of rocky, thorny, or dry soil. Where are you currently experiencing fear, anxiety, temptation, distraction, or dryness? What places in your heart find it difficult to truly receive what Jesus wants to give? Where do you need Jesus to bring rain? Run the plow? Remove rocks? Offer shade? Touch the soil? If you are willing, invite Jesus into that place and ask Him for whatever it is you most desire.

Use the space provided to write down any notes from this reflection.[14]

After your time of reflection,
slowly pray the following prayer, from Psalm 65:

You visit the earth and water it,
you greatly enrich it;
the river of God is full of water;
you provide their grain,
for so you have prepared it.

You water its furrows abundantly,
settling its ridges,
softening it with showers,
and blessing its growth.

You crown the year with your bounty;
the track of your chariot overflow with richness.

The pastures of the wilderness drip,
the hills gird themselves with joy,
the meadows clothe themselves with flocks,
the valleys deck themselves with grain,
they shout and sing together for joy.[15]

Well done, friend. Believe it or not, the exercise you just completed is in many ways one of the hardest parts of ministry leadership! In ministering to others, if we're not careful, the first thing to get set aside is often the soil of our own soul. Throughout the next few chapters, we're going to begin looking at your current baptismal preparation process—your hopes, your dreams, your realities, and your resources. As you busily tend to the field entrusted to you, you may also be tempted to avoid or neglect the soil of your own heart. If you do, we encourage you to quickly come back to the Lord (and even to this exercise) as many times as needed. Your fruitfulness in ministry is explicitly tied to your soul's own reception of grace, and since we know that you deeply desire to bear fruit, we'll make sure to remind you of this principle often.

The man who is wise, therefore, will see his life as more like a reservoir than a canal. The canal simultaneously pours out what it receives; the reservoir retains the water till it is filled, then discharges the overflow without loss to itself . . . Today there are many in the Church who act like canals, the reservoirs are far too rare . . . You too must learn to await this fullness before pouring out your gifts, do not try to be more generous than God.

—Saint Bernard of Clairvaux [16]

Your Prayer Team

In addition to tending to your own soul, it is also essential to employ others to pray for you. This is one of the most beautiful elements of the Body of Christ in action. Hidden prayers and sacrifices provide much-needed shade and protection for those, like yourself, serving in the heat of the vineyard. Prayer and fasting can and will uproot weeds, soften soil, and help new plants to thrive. If you ever need to choose between a major budget increase or ten people in Adoration for your infant baptismal preparation ministry, take the ten people in Adoration every time. Consider asking the cloistered members of the Church to pray for you, your team and the participants; it is part of their mission to pray for the Church.

If you don't already have someone praying for you in this ministry, think of one person you know who is a faithful prayer warrior. Someone who loves to spend time interceding for others. The one who, whenever you ask them to pray, you *know* will actually stop and do it. Then, reach out and ask hjm or her to pray for you, as you serve in infant baptismal preparation ministry. Make a note below of the person who came to mind, then make it a point to reach out this week! It is ideal to speak with your pastor about the prayer warriors and prayer ministries in the Church that can keep your team and the participants in their hearts. Collaborate with your pastoral ministry to invite the homebound, shut-ins, and hospitalized to pray for your team and for the participants. This has a two-fold effect of drawing them closer to and making them feel more a part of the parish, the Body of Christ, and giving them a task — their own work — to accomplish for the parish. Then, keep them updated on the struggles and victories, letting them know how they can best intercede for you, as well as the major events in the formation, especially the baptismal dates. It's essential to have your prayer warriors as part of your team before you begin your program. Do not neglect to have in place your own personal intercessor.

❈ A Note on Tasks ❈

Throughout this book, you'll find that each chapter bears a similar structure: an introduction, a brief teaching, a task or two, and a conclusion. Since it is a unique feature of these books, we'd like to make special mention of the *tasks*. Each task is part assignment, part journal entry, and part spiritual exercise. It is there to help you break open the teaching content of the chapter and apply it to your own unique situation. Each task will ask for a bit of your mind, but even more of your heart. Please note that we didn't put the tasks in each chapter as fillers to reach an arbitrary word count or provide you with busy work, just so you feel like you have something to do. Quite the opposite, in fact! Most of the chapters were built *around* a specific task. Although the teachings are important, we believe that the tasks really are the pivotal moments of each chapter, because they are the moments where you encounter the teaching for yourself and for your ministry. The tasks are where the universal becomes the personal. It's where the Holy Spirit's real work happens. We promise that if you're willing to put the work into these tasks, the return will be well worth your investment!

After being baptized by Saint John the Baptist, when Jesus came up out of the Jordan,[17] He sanctified it. Instead of the river making Him holy, He made *it* holy.[18] He parted the waters of sin and death, so all of us could pass through safely to salvation. That little baptismal font in your parish is no less holy than the Jordan River was at the very moment our Lord immersed Himself in it. To this day, in the Rite of Baptism water preserves its power to wash away sin, bestows the light of eternal life, and sweep us into the reckless love of the Father, Son, and Holy Spirit.

There's a reason, though, that the baptismal font is meant to be at the entrance of the Church. It is the door. It is the beginning. It is the gate.

But what is a gate worth if it doesn't lead anywhere?

As the first sacrament of initiation, Baptism brings us in. What we must ask ourselves is, "What does it bring us into?" In your own parish, what awaits the family members who tenderly carry their child to the font and places this little soul into the hands of the Father? Who will help them learn the voice of the Good Shepherd who has called them into the fold? Will we as a parish offer a halfhearted handshake or a high five as they pass through the revolving door of our church? Or will our parish reach out to grab their hand…and never let go?

Consider these next chapters a sounding board, offering a series of principles that encourage careful reflection: Is my current infant baptismal preparation program the best it could be in preparing God's children (that includes the whole family) to come to Him? Is the program currently a priority — both for the parish and for me? What would it look like to incorporate this book's principles into my current program?

This book will unfold the Church's guidance for parents and for parishes, who bear the great privilege and responsibility of these children both for this life and for the life to come. By considering the realities of the modern family and culture, the profound openness of new parents, the desperate need for evangelization throughout all catechesis, and the role of the whole parish in welcoming new families into the faith community, we'll work together toward a fruitful formation process, ensuring that for as beautiful as the Sacrament of Baptism is, the realities and their experience of what Baptism initiates them into is far more beautiful than they could have dreamed — eternal life in the love of the Trinity.

Saint John the Baptist, pray for us, that we might, like you, "make straight the way for the Lord." [19]

*Baptism is God's most beautiful and magnificent gift . . .
It is called gift because it is conferred on those who bring
nothing of their own; grace since it is given even to the
guilty; Baptism because sin is buried in the water; anointing
for it is priestly and royal as are those who are anointed;
enlightenment because it radiates light; clothing since it veils
our shame; bath because it washes; and seal as it is our
guard and the sign of God's Lordship.* [20]

Step One

Your Dream: A Vision for This Ministry

Medieval theologian and logician St. Thomas Aquinas was also a supporter of dreams, it seems. He says magnanimity is the soul's aspiration to bigger dreams, the jewel, or 'ornament of all the virtues,' because the magnanimous person seeks the bigger dream, and has the courage to become worthy of it. '... [M]agnanimity makes a man deem himself worthy of great things in consideration of the gifts he holds from God...' [21]

∼

Anyone who has had a baby knows about the fleeting, exciting, and terrifying moment when they realize that it is *time*. The one that is really for real. The last nine months (give or take) have been filled with waiting, planning, and dreaming.

At last, the time finally comes.

Lights on.

Deep breath.

Quick shower.

Nervous smile.

Quiet drive.

Or short walk.

To a bedroom or the hospital or a birth center.

It doesn't matter if you have done this before because each is always different. You find yourself peering into a swirl of uncertainty, fully intending to follow your carefully curated birth plan while secretly trying to prepare yourself for whatever story is actually about to unfold.

And so it begins.

She enters into her own passion. He stands at the foot of her cross. What a way to enter into the Paschal Mystery.

You labor.

For however long it takes.

Until, at last, you hear a different kind of cry.

The baby has come.

It is finished.

And yet, it has barely just begun.[22]

And alongside of the baby is this new mother and father, beloved daughter and son of God, now sharing in the mystery of His creativity and parenthood. They gave their baby their last name and now wish that the child lives also in the name of the Father and of the Son and of the Holy Spirit. They create a family below and now join with one above, building their domestic church[23] as an icon of the Most Holy Trinity, even if they have no idea that's what they're doing.

> *The celebrant asks, "What name do you give your child?"*
>
> *The parents respond with the name that they have chosen with care, the name that perhaps has great meaning within their own family, the name that encompasses all they know their child is and all they hope their child will become.*
>
> *The celebrant continues, "What do you ask of God's Church for this child?"*
>
> *The parents reply simply, "Baptism."*
>
> *And thus, this child, who has already been born, is about to be born once again.*

When parents come to the baptismal font with their child, they are surrendering that child into the water as a "burial into Christ's death." [24] The water of death and the grave that all of us have inherited from our first parents: sin. The water of hope in the Resurrection that we have received from Christ empowering the baptismal waters and raising from the tomb on Easter morning. Whether or not these new parents are fully cognitive of this reality changes nothing about what is really happening. In that moment there is only hope and trust. Simply openness. Nothing can interfere with what is happening or the grace being poured out.

Even in their most limited understanding of what they are engaging in, God honors the level of trust that has been placed in the arms of His Church, His sacraments, His Heart. He will hold nothing back from this child or from their parents.

> *It is Jesus in fact that you seek when you dream of happiness; He is waiting for you when nothing else you find satisfies you; He is the beauty to which you are so attracted; it is He Who provokes you with that thirst for fullness that will not let you settle for compromise; it is He Who urges you to shed the masks of a false life; it is He Who reads in your hearts your most genuine choices, the choices that others try to stifle.*

> *It is Jesus Who stirs in you the desire to do something great with your lives, the will to follow an ideal, the refusal to allow yourselves to be grounded down by mediocrity, the courage to commit yourselves humbly and patiently to improving yourselves and society, making the world more human and more fraternal.* [25]

Baptism is a sacrament of hopes and dreams, because it is a sacrament of new beginnings. And to every new beginning we bring our hopes and dreams, even if they seem completely unrealistic and naïve. In taking on the infant Baptism preparation process in your parish, you are in your own new beginning. Yes, the Lord called you to this particular plot in the vineyard for a reason, but there's also a reason that *you* said "yes." As with any spiritual father- or mother-to-be, there is a vision in your heart for what this ministry can become, what its fruit can look and taste like, and what the impact can be in your own parish community. You may know the excitement (and nervousness!) of preparing your materials, checking the attendance list, and waiting for families to arrive for your first gathering.

Of course, if you've served in baptismal preparation for more than one day, you may also know that, as beautiful as birth and Baptism are in theory, it's possible you're staring down a baptismal preparation program that couldn't be farther from your dreams! Perhaps you inherited a program from the catechetical leader who came before you. Maybe the majority of parents approaching you to request Baptism can hardly articulate why, or the ones who can have reasons that are, shall we say, less than compelling: "It's a nice tradition we wanted to continue," "Grandma will kill us if we don't baptize her grandchild," and "Better safe than sorry, right?" You do your best to give these parents a lifetime of catechesis in a handful of classes, because you have it on good authority that they'll disappear after the Baptism . . . at least until their child inevitably shows up for First Communion seven years down the road. (And since we're assuming you might be in charge of that, too, you know in the back of your mind you'll also carry the added responsibility of trying to catch them up on everything they missed).

Your Dream: A Vision for This Ministry

When it feels like you're fighting a never-ending uphill battle, it can be hard enough to keep from feeling jaded, much less muster up a great deal of enthusiasm for the whole baptismal preparation process.

But.

What if things could be different?

What if, even if you couldn't change the types of parents who came to you seeking Baptism, you could connect with them in a truly meaningful way? What if your baptismal preparation was something that new families *wanted* to participate in? What if you could be part of what God desired to do in the lives of these new families? What if this sacrament and the preparation that went with it became a powerful catalyst for personal and spiritual growth in each new family? What if this was just the beginning and not the end of your time with them? What if your parish became known as the place where families who baptized babies stayed long after the Baptism was over? What if you could be the hands and feet of Christ, reaching out to new parents and drawing them into the community of the Church? What if something that feels like a lost cause is really a golden moment? What if, at Baptism, we grabbed onto the hands of these new families and then never let go?

What could . . . no, what *would* be different?

❁ Task: The Dream ❁

For this task, we want you to spend a bit of time *hoping and dreaming* about your baptismal preparation process. If you're just beginning in baptismal preparation, this will probably be easy! If you've been at it for a while, this may be a bit more challenging. After all, when we get stuck in survival mode or discouraged at the reality of our situation, the first thing we often forget to do is dream. (Nobody has time for that, right?) Soon enough, if we don't know where we're going, pretty much any road will suffice.

"Would you tell me, please, which way I ought to go from here?"

"That depends a good deal on where you want to get to," said the Cat.

"I don't much care where," said Alice.

"Then it doesn't matter which way you go," said the Cat.

"So long as I get somewhere," Alice added as an explanation.

"Oh, you're sure to do that," said the Cat,

"if you only walk long enough."

–Lewis Caroll [26]

Before we can talk about the right path, we need to dream about the proper destination. When a couple is preparing to welcome a new baby into their lives, their hearts are filled with dreams — for their home, their family, their child, their future. They know there will be detours along the way, but that doesn't stop them (nor should it) from painting a picture of the vision burning within their heart. Now, you get to do the same thing!

Set aside the reality of whatever your current circumstances look like and think outside the box. If you had unlimited time, unlimited resources, and permission to build a baptismal preparation program of your dreams, what would it look like? What would happen? How long would the process last? Who would lead it? (Don't worry if you don't know anyone like that in the parish). Who would help? How would you welcome families? How would you catechize families? Even more importantly, *after* a family went through this process, what would they be doing? How would they be living? What would their home life look like? What would their spiritual lives look like? How would they be connected to the parish? What would they desire? What do *you* desire? Rest your head against the Good Shepherd, stare up at the clouds, and dream together. This isn't the time for ". . . but that won't work" or ". . . how in the world would we make that happen?" This is the time to hope and dream. It doesn't have to be realistic or practical.

Use the space below to answer each question. You may be as detailed or as brief as you like, but we encourage you to give each question at least a few minutes of your time. From our experience, we know you've probably already been thinking or daydreaming about these things, but *incarnating* it in a tangible way is a large part of what will make your journey through this book worthwhile. Go ahead and dream with the Holy Spirit.

Imagine you had unlimited time, unlimited resources, and permission to build a baptismal preparation program of your dreams ... then answer each question below:

After a family went through your ideal process, what would they be doing? How would they be living? What would their home life look like? What would their spiritual lives look like? How would they be connected to the parish? What would they desire?

How would you welcome families? When would you gather? Where and how would you meet? What would make it good, true, and beautiful?

Who would lead it? (Don't worry if you don't know anyone like that in the parish right now). Who would help? Who would be involved? What kind of people would they be?

How long would the process last? How would you catechize families? What would it look like? What would happen? What would *not* happen?

Use this last space below to write or sketch any ideas, images, words, phrases, smells, tastes, sights, sounds, Scriptures, saints, or quotations that come to mind or heart when you think about your dream baptismal preparation process:

Your Dream: A Vision for This Ministry

How are you feeling after sketching out your dreams? Was it easy? Difficult? Enlightening? Frustrating? Clarifying? Even if it felt a bit "pie in the sky," the time you just spent articulating your hopes for your ministry was far from a waste. It wasn't even just a "nice exercise," so that you had something to do in this chapter. Quite the opposite. It was a small participation in the mystery of the Creator and His creative love. The One Who brings something out of nothing. The God Who, ". . . infinitely perfect and blessed in himself, in a plan of sheer goodness freely created man to make him share in his own blessed life." [27] The God of all hopefulness.

For now, you may take the excellent work you've just completed and set it aside until we reach the next chapter. We'll return to it then, because our hopes and dreams actually reveal our deepest desires. And over time, as we dig into our hearts and peel off layers of superficial wanting, we find that our desires become purer. Holier. This is true both for us and for the parents and families we are ministering to. Beginning with, growing, and shaping our own desire for ministry is what prepares us to walk with parents and families, helping them, as their initial, surface desire for the Sacrament of Baptism (for example, "because Grandma insists") has the potential to be reshaped and transformed into something purer (for example, a desire to become like Christ).

For example, consider the growth of desire that occurs within the Sacrament of Matrimony. A man and woman vow to love each other until death . . . a vow full of hopes and dreams, and a little (or a lot) of naivety! This makes sense. It has not yet withstood the heat and storms of love that will be sure to follow in years to come. The Rite of Matrimony affirms this in the blessing that follows the vows, "May the Lord in his kindness *strengthen the consent* you have declared before the Church." [28] That is the grace of the Sacrament of Matrimony — grace that eagerly begins with infant hopes and dreams, slowly maturing them into the formidable fire of adult desire, the desire that has been tested and tried . . . and yet, continues to burn.

Similarly, this is the grace of Baptism. Baptism is a Sacrament of Initiation. It is the first of a series of three Sacraments of Initiation that take place over the course of several years for many children. It is meant to be the *beginning* of a journey. A Sacrament of Initiation, not one of completion. This is true not just for the child, but for the entire family, as well. "The faith required for Baptism is not a perfect and mature faith, but a beginning that is called to develop." [29] When we look back at the many families we've all encountered, the amount of faith (or lack thereof) that many of them bring should not plunge us into frustration or discouragement, but rather should nudge us back to the beginning.

❈ Task: Anchored by Hope ❈

As we conclude, we ask you to complete a brief but powerful meditation. The winds and rains of ministry can often dampen our own hope, leaving us at times discouraged, or perhaps even despairing. If that has not been the case for you yet, you may find yourself there in the future. For this exercise, allow the Holy Spirit to lift your spirit as you reflect upon the following paragraph on *Hope* from the *Catechism of the Catholic Church*. To begin, find a quiet space. Then read through this paragraph once in its entirety, slowly and receptively:

The virtue of hope responds to the aspiration to happiness which God has placed in the heart of every man; it takes up the hopes that inspire men's activities and purifies them so as to order them to the Kingdom of heaven; it keeps man from discouragement; it sustains him during times of abandonment; it opens up his heart in expectation of eternal beatitude. Buoyed up by hope, he is preserved from selfishness and led to the happiness that flows from charity ... through the merits of Jesus Christ and of his Passion, God keeps us in the "hope that does not disappoint." Hope is the "sure and steadfast anchor of the soul ... that enters ... where Jesus has gone as a forerunner on our behalf." Hope is also a weapon that protects us in the struggle of salvation: "Let us ... put on the breastplate of faith and charity, and for a helmet the hope of salvation." It affords us joy even under trial: "Rejoice in your hope, be patient in tribulation." Hope is expressed and nourished in prayer, especially in the Our Father, the summary of everything that hope leads us to desire. [30]

After your initial reading, go back to the passage again, this time paying attention to whichever analogy for hope resonates most with you, circling or underlining it (for example, a buoy, an anchor, a weapon, a breastplate, and so on). Then, ask the Holy Spirit to show you the deeper meaning of that metaphor for your own soul. For example, if hope is an anchor, that makes it the deepest thing, something that begins at the surface, but ultimately rests in the depths. Which metaphor speaks to you personally? What is the Holy Spirit saying to you through it? Spend a few moments contemplating this.

When you are ready, return to the passage a third time, letting the Lord's encouragement sink into your spirit and console any areas in need of His divine hopefulness.

Your Dream: A Vision for This Ministry

The Lord's deep hope needs to take root in our hearts not only for our own sake, but also for the sake of our ministerial fruitfulness. With families coming to us for baptismal preparation, it takes effort to forge relationships and create an environment where their little seed of desire (something a heavy rain or cold wind would crush) can grow into a mighty oak of discipleship (something that barely moves against the wind and rain). An environment that meets the deepest and most personal needs of parents at a time when their entire life has changed. An environment that makes them want to come back, so we have more time to teach deeper things when they're ready. If we, the Church — the People of Christ anchored in hope — meet these needs, build relationships of trust, and minister to their fears and desires in this golden moment of their life — they will return for more.

And little by little we could know them. And they would want to be known more.

Little by little we could evangelize them. And they would return for more life in Christ.

Little by little we could catechize them. And they would come back, because it is home.

This may seem as if it will take a long time. It will. It's supposed to. We aren't *given* time with a family. We *make* time with a family. We make it every time that we incarnate the love and truth of Christ by properly ministering to the needs of the moment for these parents. It's not magic. It's ministry. It's helping each person and each family receive the everlasting love of the Blessed Trinity.

And *that* is the real dream.

FIELD NOTES—
with Sister Hyacinthe Defos du Rau, OP

"In the time we're living now, we have a massive deprivation of hope. Suicide. Depression. Abortion. Or the fact that a lot of people convert to faith and then give up after a while. Those demonstrate lack of hope, more than anything else. Giving up is basically what not having hope looks like. It is possible to have faith without hope. It is possible to say, 'Yes, I believe everything the Church says is true. But it's not for me. I will never be a saint. I will never get to heaven.' There's a constant discourse from the Church and the world on what we should be doing and morally how we should be acting. In catechesis, we're very good at giving the map, giving the end, and giving the requirements of charity. 'This is what a holy person needs to do.' But charity without hope is a massive burden.

Christianity so often sounds like a message of despair, this perfect message which cannot possibly be for me, because 'look at me! I'm unable to get myself out of the sin I'm currently in the grips of. I'm unable to be as I think I should be in the eyes of God.' We are very poor at encouraging hope. What if we dared to say, 'You know, if you're imperfect, it's a common, normal experience of Christian life. Failure is absolutely part of it. Sin is part of the Christian experience, a common part.' I think a lot more people are not in the Church because of lack of hope, not lack of faith." [31]

Your Dream: A Vision for This Ministry

Step Two

God's Dream: Come to the Waters

Just as a man with his wife begets legitimate sons and daughters, so Christ [begets children] with the Church his spouse. "The seed is the word of God." (Luke 8:11) Therefore, we Christians are all children of God, of the king Christ and the queen, the Church. [32]

~

IN THE PREVIOUS CHAPTER, YOU SPENT A GREAT DEAL OF TIME identifying and articulating your hopes and dreams for a baptismal preparation process. Now, with that vision nestled safely in your heart, we'll turn toward the Author of all dreams for divine guidance in our ministerial task. In this chapter, we'll ask, "What is *God's* vision for infant baptismal preparation as given to Mother Church? What are *His* hopes and dreams for how parents and their children are ushered into the family of God? What does the *Church* most desire that all parishes, priests, and leaders remember for this area of ministry?" After all, this is His vineyard, and it would befit us to first seek His plans for yielding the most fruitful harvest. As we explore these questions and their accompanying answers, we will surely seek God's desires; but as the Holy Spirit dwells inside of you, too, don't be surprised if you find that God's dreams and your dreams have a great deal in common.

REQUIRED RESOURCE

The Catechism of the Catholic Church, paragraphs 1213–1284 — the source for all essential teachings related to the Sacrament of Baptism. If you don't have a copy, this is the perfect time to find or order one. A parish catechetical leader's library isn't complete without it!

RECOMMENDED RESOURCE

Instruction on Infant Baptism (*Pastoralis actio*). A magisterial[33] document on Baptism released by the Sacred Congregation for the Doctrine of the Faith in 1980. It is an aerial look at the doctrines followed by general guidelines for pastoral care for this sacrament. You can find it on the Vatican website: www.vatican.va

❧ Task: God's Dream ❧

Let's begin this chapter by reading the *Catechism of the Catholic Church's* introduction to the Sacrament of Baptism, given in paragraph 1213. The *Catechism* contains the Church's account of this sacrament given to us for every parish across the world, and thus, the essential content to which we are all called to be faithful. This brief introductory paragraph is the key to discovering God's desire for Baptism. Take a few minutes to read this paragraph now. As you do, try to glean God's Heart for families seeking to baptize their child. What does He most desire? Sketch out two to three points in the space below, using active language to finish the prompt, "In Baptism, God desires to…"

Now that you've made your own observations, we'll expand upon them throughout this next chapter. Although that may have felt like a simplistic exercise, you'd be surprised at how often we as parish catechetical leaders move forward with program planning before ever consulting the Heart of Christ. To know what God wants for the Sacrament of Baptism (or for any sacrament), we don't need to set off on a theological wild goose chase or make our best educated guess. He is not hiding His will in some place we would never think to look. The Lord wants us to seek, but He also wants to be found and known. Through Divine Revelation — the Person of His Son, Jesus Christ, and the teachings of the Church handed on and safeguarded by the Magisterium, He has already told us what He most deeply desires. God's hopes and dreams for the Sacrament of Baptism are contained within the doctrine of what the sacrament actually *does*. As "the gateway to life in the Spirit" and "the door which gives access to the other sacraments," [34] Baptism marks entry into a new life. With the Catechism as our guide, let's open that door and see where it takes us.

Note: In this next section, we're going to read through the *Catechism's* presentation on Baptism. To make this easier to digest, we've broken these readings down into three smaller sections. However, if you prefer to read the entire presentation at once, you may go ahead and do that now (paragraphs 1214–1274).

❊ Task: Read & Write ❊

In Baptism, God desires to . . .
free us from sin (see CCC 1213)

Before continuing, read the *Catechism of the Catholic Church*, paragraphs 1214–1228. As you read, feel free to write down any notes in the space below.

When the priest pours water over the child's head, we picture invisible stains of sin being washed away and the parents trusting that through faith and obedience their child will be cleansed from the sin that plagues all humanity. But there's another image that speaks far more carnally, one often forgotten by our modern custom of pouring water over a person's head. Throughout much of Church history, those baptized were fully submerged under the waters (remember from our *Catechism* reading that the Greek word for baptize means "to 'plunge' or 'immerse'" [35]). This certainly could recall images of washing away sin, but to the Jews (and all of the ancient world) water meant something quite different.

Our 21st century Christian eyes see water through the lens of Christ's redeeming work. Christ transformed water into wine. Christ empowered the baptismal waters. Christ poured water and blood from His side, when He conquered death on the cross.[36] However, the cultures stemming from ancient Mesopotamia saw water in a more ominous way. The *Catechism* notes that water, particularly the sea, represented death.[37] The unknown, chaos. This imagery was common in religions surrounding God's chosen people — Akkadian, Sumerian, Philistine, Assyrian, and Babylonian, among others. The Jews were no exception.

The *Catechism* continues with the story. In the Genesis creation account, water is the image of the unformed world, "'overshadowed' by the Spirit of God." [38] Then, God speaks, drawing order from the unformed world and birthing our universe, our world, and us. When the world returned to sin, it was engulfed into the primal chaos of the flood and only Noah and his family were delivered from the destruction in the Ark.[39] When Pharoah called for the slaughter of the Hebrew sons, one baby boy is saved from the waters of the Nile by his own tiny ark, a basket of reed and pitch. Later, this baby, Moses, would lead God's people from slavery in Egypt toward the Promised Land. But death was not done with them. Pharoah pursued with his chariots. As the Jews fled, they became trapped between the blades of Egypt and the depths of the Red Sea. It looked like the waters of Exodus would be the death of their people: the final tomb for the offspring of Abraham, Isaac, and Jacob.

And then, the waters parted, and instead of death and destruction, the Hebrews tread unharmed on a wide-open path. As the last of God's Chosen

People stepped onto the far banks of the sea, the Hebrews looked back to see the pursuing army on the same path through the parted waters — not in obedience, but in defiance of God's will. In that moment, the waters crashed down on those who would oppose God, and the sin of Egypt was returned to the chaos of the deep. The Red Sea was a tomb, after all. A tomb where sin was laid to rest. And as the children of Abraham were freed from Pharoah through water, we are freed from sin through the waters of Baptism. [40]

These are the stark images that were present in the minds of the first priests, laity, and converts when they surrendered to the waters of Baptism. It is *this* picture they embraced when they were laid to rest under the deep. It is *this* story they professed, when they obeyed the call to be baptized. It is a portrait Saint Paul himself would paint in his *Letter to the Romans*:

> *Do you not know that all of us who have been baptized into Christ Jesus were baptized into his death? We were buried therefore with him by baptism into death, so that as Christ was raised from the dead by the glory of the Father, we too might walk in newness of life.*[41]

It is a parallel that Saint Ambrose would emphasize: ". . . [S]ee where Baptism comes from, if not from the cross of Christ, from his death." [42] Baptism is our first resurrection and it is also our first martyrdom.

So why the emphasis on the macabre in a book about a sweet ceremony with family, friends, and babies clad in white? Because proper understanding of these baptismal images makes a world of difference for how we prepare for it, how we prepare the parents to view it, and more importantly, how we prepare ourselves to view the *parents*. When parents come to the baptismal font, they surrender their child into the water — the water of death all of us inherited from our first parents *and* the water of hope in the Resurrection we received from Christ rising from the burial cloths on Easter morning. They lay their child into the tomb of the abyss and the arms of the Church at the same time. This is an amazing moment for the child, and it's also a defining moment for mom and dad.

Because many parents don't comprehend the full ramifications of our last few paragraphs, what they *do* understand is that the world they've just brought a child into is very broken — a reason often given for not having children at all. Block it out as we may, no one needs convincing that this world is plagued with anxiety, abuse, broken families, trauma, pandemics, poverty, cancer, disasters, and death — universally and personally. Even more problematic than our physical maladies are the interior sicknesses slowly deteriorating our hearts, minds, and souls, putting us at war with each other . . . and with our very own selves. We're familiar with the enemy, aware that the prince of this world "prowls around like a roaring lion, seeking someone to devour." [43] The devil brings only suffering and death, in this life and in the life to come. And thanks to original sin, we're his prisoners.

This is what God desires to free us from. Through the saving death and Resurrection of His Son, Jesus Christ, and through His personal encounter and relationship with us, God ransoms us back. The *Catechism* reminds us that the baptismal exorcisms signify "liberation from sin and from its instigator the devil." [44] In the child being baptized, not only does He desire to erase the stain of original sin, but also to immunize the child against the ongoing decay of the human soul. In the parent, He desires the kind of faith that would lay their son or daughter on the altar of death, reasoning — like Mary or Abraham — that even if God did not spare their child, He could still raise them from the dead.[45]

❈ Task: Read & Write ❈

*In Baptism, God desires to . . . give us new birth
as sons and daughters of God (CCC 1213)*

Before continuing, read the *Catechism of the Catholic Church*, paragraphs 1246–1266. As you read, feel free to write down any notes in the space below.

You don't need to be around the westernized world very long before you pick up on its penchant for "pulling ourselves up by our bootstraps," ironic as that impossible task may be. We are very good at earning things, but we are very bad at receiving things. At least, we *become* very bad at receiving things after a lifetime reminds us "there's no such thing as a free lunch." Maybe, that's why Baptism is so attractive, even for those who are not actively practicing the faith. Perhaps it ignites something primal in our being. Something that longs to receive, to be seen, to be cared for, to be given all that we need without having anything to give. "All you who are thirsty, come to the water! You who have no money, come, buy grain and eat." [46]

There is nowhere this is more obvious than at Baptism.

A helpless infant, who can do absolutely nothing on her own except cry out, is brought before the baptismal font. Entrusted to parents and godparents, who speak on her behalf and bestow a new birthright, while she sleeps. She has done nothing other than let herself be carried here, and even against that she has little ability to resist. Here, she simply receives the grace poured into her soul — the *Catechism* calls this the "sheer gratuitousness of the grace of salvation." [47]

Although infants cannot yet profess personal faith, this "does not prevent the Church from conferring this sacrament on them, since in reality it is in Her own faith that She baptizes them." [48] This point of doctrine was clearly defined by Saint Augustine:

> *When children are presented to be given spiritual grace, . . . it is not so much those holding them in their arms who present them — although, if these people are good Christians they are included among those who present the children — as the whole company of saints and faithful Christians. . . . It is done by the whole of Mother Church which is in the saints, since it is as a whole that she gives birth to each and every one of them.*[49]

Given the distress some parents face when they've tried to give their children a Christian upbringing only to watch them abandon the faith, "some pastors are asking themselves whether they should not be stricter before admitting infants to Baptism." [50] Some think it better to delay Baptism in favor of a longer preparation period. Others believe the sacrament should be put off until that child can make the choice for themselves. And though there are certainly pastoral considerations, this is the same error that has been recycled for centuries. Throughout the Middle Ages, several councils (Council of Vienne 1311–1312, Council of Florence 1431–1449, Council of Trent 1545–1563, and so on), the Protestant Reformation and its various rejections of infant Baptism (or at very least its sacramental efficacy), the twentieth century, and up to today, the Church has never wavered in her defense of infant Baptism. Rather, it has been reaffirmed and defended.

Over. And over. And over again.

The Church is not defending a finer philosophical preference. Instead, She is insisting that Baptism is not something we earn or prove ourselves worthy of. It is something we *receive*. God Himself does the acting, the saving, the adopting, not only the "forgiveness of sins but also the granting of grace and the virtues." [51] We only need to wholeheartedly consent. There are nuances and limitations we can consider later, but the *Catechism* is adamant that the Church would no sooner refuse Baptism to the smallest child than a mother would refuse milk to her newborn, because he cannot yet form words to say he is hungry. In the Sacrament of Baptism, God desires that parents who have transmitted natural life to this child would now fully awaken their vocation to also become mothers and fathers in faith.[52]

"If it is understood this way, the practice of infant Baptism is truly evangelical, since it has the force of witness, manifesting God's initiative and the gratuitous character of the love with which He surrounds our lives: 'not that we loved God but that he loved us . . .'" [53] We love, because He first loved us. Even in the case of adults, the demands that the reception of Baptism involves should not make us forget that "he saved us, not because of deeds done by us in righteousness, but in virtue of his own mercy, by the washing of regeneration and renewal in the Holy Spirit." [54] In Baptism, all of us become newly born.

❈ Task: Read & Write ❈

In Baptism, God desires to . . . incorporate us into the Church and invite us to share Her mission[55]

Before continuing, read the *Catechism of the Catholic Church*, paragraphs 1229–1245 and 1267–1274. As you read, feel free to write down any notes in the space below.

If a newborn baby were left to fend for itself, it would die in less than twenty-four hours. The spiritual life isn't all that much different. The necessary care isn't profound. Rather, an infant demands small things, on an extremely consistent basis. Eat. Sleep. Cry. Be held. Repeat. Again. And again. And again. Thanks be to God, our heavenly Father assumes responsibility for parenting His children. And He. Does. Not. Fail.

But.

He also desires to accomplish this work within the womb of the Church. He desires that *we* are an active part of nurturing the newly born in faith. The *Catechism* uses the word "incorporate," [56] meaning "to unite or work into something already existent, so as to form an indistinguishable whole." [57] According to Saint Vincent Ferrer, ". . . [A]fter Baptism parents ought to consider themselves as nurses of the child of Christ the King." [58] This need for the community to nurture the newly baptized is affirmed repeatedly in the *Catechism*:

- "By its very nature, infant Baptism requires a *post-baptismal catechumenate* . . . for the necessary flowering of baptismal grace in personal growth." [59]

- "Baptism is the sacrament of faith. But faith needs the community of believers." [60]

- "For all the baptized, children or adults, faith must grow *after* Baptism." [61]

- "For the grace of Baptism to unfold, the parents' help is important. So too is the role of the *godfather* and *godmother* . . ." [62]

- "The whole ecclesial community bears some responsibility for the development and safeguarding of the grace given at Baptism." [63]

The period of time following Baptism is theologically and developmentally significant for both parents and child. However, it isn't the time to deeply expound on Saint Thomas Aquinas's *Summa Theologicae*. It may not even be the time to dig into the *Catechism*. What should we focus on? Simple things. Attachment and relationship to Jesus Christ — the Good Shepherd, God — the Good Father, the Holy Spirit — the Comforter, and Mary, our Mother. Learning — not just in our brains, but in our very being — that just like Mom or Dad runs to you when you're hungry or scared in the middle of the night, God Himself comes swiftly whenever we are in need. Learning that just like you belong in your family, we belong in our family of faith. Learning that just like we are loved unconditionally by your parents, we are also loved unconditionally by God our Father.

In this time, personal relationships within the community of faith are crucial, largely because they are a taste of the infinite love and shared communion of the Trinity. Within this community, the newly baptized along with their parents and families can be spoon fed "the pure spiritual milk" [64] of the Word in small amounts, extremely consistently, as they experience the love, care, and nurture of the Body of Christ. Over time, the newly baptized will then learn to share in the mission of the Church and embrace new spiritual identities, always rooted as son or daughter, then layering on identities of brother or sister, husband or wife, and father or mother, fully able to "participate in the apostolic and missionary activity of the People of God." [65]

Good, bad, or nonexistent, whatever our parishes are or aren't offering families following Baptism will set the tone for your parish's ministry to children and families throughout their entire lifetime. And just as infants are soft, squishy, and extremely impressionable, "infant" parents bring hearts with clay still wet and malleable for formation and relationship building — with the Blessed Trinity and with your parish, the Body of Christ. May we make our ministerial work *easier* by taking advantage of this fertile ground.

❈ Task: Side by Side ❈

As we conclude this chapter, we encourage you to read through the whole *Catechism* section on Baptism, paragraphs 1214–1274, once more in its entirety. You may find that it reads differently now. If you do choose to read it again, note anything that strikes you. Allow yourself to be puzzled, confirmed, challenged, encouraged, inspired, or all of the above. Knowingly or unknowingly, this content is what all your future catechesis will draw from.

For the bulk of this task, now that you have a clearer picture of God's dream for baptismal preparation, page back a few chapters in this book and reminisce over the hopes and dreams *you* initially sketched out for your infant baptismal preparation process. (If you're able to do this in a quiet chapel with the Blessed Sacrament, even better.) Take note of how your dreams compare to God's dreams, as fleshed out in this chapter. Getting on God's page takes us time, and that's to be expected. Plenty of things may be different, but right now we only *want you to focus on what is the same*. Where do your heart and God's Heart beat in perfect rhythm? Where do you see eye to eye? What hopes and dreams do you share? Spend a few moments in prayer and reflection, making note of anything you and God share in the space provided.

Excellent work! We've asked a great deal from you in this chapter, so now we'd like you set aside this book, take a break, and refill your own body and spirit. If you like, go back to the task from our introduction chapter on page 15, asking the Holy Spirit to water the soil of your soul once again. Or, in keeping with the theme of this book, you could also choose to spend some time in, on, or near *water*. Let cool water pour over your hands a few minutes longer the next time you wash them. Or, you could even draw yourself a hot bath, take a dip in a refreshing pool, drive up north to your cabin on the lake, soak in a hot tub, stroll barefoot on the sand of a salty ocean beach, take a boat ride, walk along the bank of a river... Close your eyes and remember the moment when God the Father tenderly poured His holy water over you, His beloved son or daughter, even if you were an infant then. See, hear, touch, smell, feel what the water is telling you about your being. Meditate on the element itself. Why did God choose water for this sacrament? Primal. Powerful. Raw. Floating on the chaos of turmoil and death. Refreshing. Lifegiving. The sound of bringing in new life and new birth. Before diving into strategies for ministering to others, first feel your own soul refreshed and refilled. Let something new be born in you once again.

FIELD NOTES—with Dr. Martha Drennan

"Baptism is more about what we lack that God supplies in the sacrament than it is about what God takes away. God makes you His children. He puts you in His family. God is your Father; you are His child. Of all the things a parent knows on a natural level about having children, God is doing it on a supernatural level in Baptism." [66]

Step Three

The Rite Stuff: Church Teaching

The liturgy is the prime way the catechist should think about teaching the faith. Inserting participants into the liturgy is equivalent to beginning to insert them into eternity. [67]

∼

Say you want to travel to New York City, but you live in Pittsburgh. (For our friends outside of the continental United States, that's just shy of 400 miles distance by car). If you're using your odometer to judge success, then when the numbers read 400 miles higher than when you started, you could say you've reached your destination, right? Until you look up at the sign, as you enter the city and see Louisville, Kentucky. Or Winston-Salem, North Carolina. Or Chicago, Illinois. All are approximately 400 miles from the New York City, but none of them are where you wanted to end up. You get the point. Simply putting on mileage isn't enough. When setting out on any journey — a catechetical one included — it's important for us to begin with our end in mind, plotting out a path that will take us safely to our desired destination.

This is just as true when we approach sacramental preparation. For Mother Church, every sacrament contains a "map" within the liturgy of the sacramental rite itself. Liturgy is not only *one* way in which we enter into God's divine life — it is the *primary* way in which He offers and in which we receive His grace. Although programs and curricula can be immensely helpful (we'll even recommend some later in this book), the Church never expects that we would purchase them, in order to bear fruit in ministry. The Church has already given us a universal instruction manual for nurturing spiritual children. Through the liturgy, believe it or not, we really do have all we need.

> **REQUIRED RESOURCE**
>
> **The Order of Baptism for Children, 2020 edition** — A hardcover book that probably lives in the parish sacristy and smells like chrism. This contains both pastoral guidelines, as well as the ritual text for the Rite of Baptism itself. For editions printed outside of the United States, paragraph numbers may vary slightly. You'll find it necessary to have a hard copy of this text in front of you, as you work through the tasks in this chapter. You can purchase your own copy **here** [insert link] or speak with your pastor about borrowing a copy from your parish. (if you are the pastor, this should be very easy for you!)

Baptism 101: The Rite Stuff

How do we know what parents or godparents truly need to learn before their child is baptized? This is where the liturgy comes in handy. For Baptism, as in all sacraments, liturgy is central in considering what to teach and when to teach it. The ritual text guides us in what material should be included in any catechesis that either precedes or follows reception of the stages in preparing for the sacrament. There are two components to this:

- Teaching *to* the rite means looking at the questions and answers within the rite itself, ensuring that our teaching gives participants what they need to respond with understanding and conviction, when they participate in the liturgy. After all, what we don't want is for parents or godparents to speak these words without being able to give their authentic, wholehearted consent.

- Teaching *from* the rite means looking at the proclamations and intercessions that are contained within the rite, identifying what the Church prays for the participants to experience in the next part of the process (suggesting that there is indeed supposed be a "next part" of the process!) Her expressed hope helps shape our catechesis in the next stage of their journey.[68]

Because Baptism is an encounter with God and His grace, teaching to and from the rite helps us prepare a participant to appreciate the grace they are about to receive. The rite shouldn't limit or stifle our catechesis, but instead should inspire it and is the sure means of entering into what God intends for this sacrament. Ideally, teaching to and from the rites does not mean we give parents and godparents a script, so they can study the rites and follow along. Rather, it means that the catechist — knowing the rite inside and out — shapes his or her catechesis to help the participants more fully enter into the rites when they take place.[69] In other words, effective catechesis doesn't give a person the map to navigate for themselves. Instead, it invites them to hop in the car and embark on an adventure . . . together.

Task: Practice Teaching *To* or *From* the Rite of Baptism

Now that you understand the theory, let's get behind the wheel and go for a metaphorical drive. For this task, you'll need the *Order of Baptism of Children*. There are many variations of the baptismal rite, both within and outside of Mass. For simplicity's sake, we'll use the "Order of Baptism for One Child" (Chapter 2), which contains several sections:

- Rite of Receiving the Child
- Sacred Celebration of the Word of God
  - Biblical Readings and Homily
  - Prayer of the Faithful
  - Prayer of Exorcism and Anointing before Baptism
- Celebration of Baptism
  - Blessing of Water and Invocation of God over the Water
  - Renunciation of Sin and Profession of Faith
  - Baptism
- Explanatory Rites
  - Anointing after Baptism
  - Clothing with a White Garment
  - Handing On of a Lighted Candle
  - "Ephphatha"
- Conclusion of the Rite
  - Lord's Prayer
  - Blessing and Dismissal

For example, in the "Rite of Receiving the Child," the celebrant asks the parents of the child, "What do you ask of God's Church for [child's name]?" The parents respond "Baptism," although the text indicates that they may also use other words (e.g. "Faith," "The grace of Christ," "Entrance into the Church" or "Eternal life,") This portion of the text is fertile ground for catechists who know how to direct their teaching to the content of the upcoming rite. We can ask ourselves: What is assumed by this simple liturgical exchange about what the parents would have been taught prior to it? They would need to have been taught about the nature of the Church, Her sacraments and the Sacrament of Baptism, in particular. Why do we ask for Baptism from "God's Church," rather than directly from God? They would have to have been taught about eternal life. What is eternity? How is it attained or lost? Why is it offered by God in the first place? If the parents are to fully enter into the baptismal liturgy, a certain (yet not comprehensive) understanding of these things is necessary.

Or let's look at another example, like the prayer over the mother and father from the "Blessing and Dismissal" section. The celebrant asks God to "bless the father of this child, so that, together with his wife, they may, by word and example, prove to be the first witnesses of the faith to their child." [70] We can ask ourselves: What is the Church's hope for this child's upbringing and family life? There may be obstacles or challenges that stand in the way of the parents living this out together. What kind of support is needed, if they are married? If they are not married? What does the word "witness" mean? How are the parents of this child enabled to witness to their child "by word and example?" If the parents are to truly experience the fruit of the Church's hopes and prayers after Baptism, a particular kind of help and support is necessary here.

Now it's your turn! In the *Order of Baptism of Children*, turn to the "Renunciation of Sin," which occurs immediately prior to Baptism. Read the second option. It asks three questions. We'll focus on the second question: "Do you renounce the lure of evil, so that sin may have no mastery over you?" This question may seem straightforward at first, but it actually offers ample opportunity to "teach to the rite."

The first step in teaching to the rite is meditating upon the deep meaning we often find compressed into just a few words. Consider these questions. What is evil? Why does the text refer to the "lure of evil"? Is evil alluring? If so, why? What is deceptively attractive about evil? Why would anyone be allured by something evil? Consider your own spiritual life. Have you ever been "lured" by evil? To what result? Why does the Church ask, "Do you refuse to be mastered by sin?" Why not simply ask, "Do you refuse to sin?" What is the difference between these two sentences. What does it mean to be "mastered"? Could this be a reference to master and slave? Does the notion of slavery bring to mind any particular Scripture passages?

Second, choose a Scripture that speaks to the battle against sin. For example, read Matthew 4:1–11, the temptation of Jesus. Read through the passage slowly. If you like, devote fifteen minutes to a brief meditation of this passage.

Third, ask the Holy Spirit to enlighten your intellect. You are about to prepare a simple plan for a teaching on the renunciation of sin, specifically on the question, "Do you renounce the lure of evil, so that sin may have no mastery over you?" Ask the Lord to show you the insights He wishes to share with your parents preparing for their child's Baptism. Spend some time in prayer before the last step to focus on Christ being the center and attraction of the teaching and the needs of the parents that you have learned from being with them.

Lastly, using the space below, write out the main points of your teaching. You can do this in bullet points, or in a written-out script. Try to include at least one to two references to the *Catechism of the Catholic Church* and one to two references to Scripture. Although you may indeed present this teaching at some point, remember that the goal here is *your* own formation. The last part of this task may seem laborious, but pulling these pieces together is the very thing that develops finesse and depth in your catechetical leadership. Please sketch out your teaching in the space below.

That task was a big one! In retrospect, how difficult was the exercise for you to complete? If it was your first time moving through a task like this, it may have been challenging or tedious. With more practice and repetition, you'll find that this process becomes second nature, something you can do with ease. We recommend moving through this exercise multiple times, with different sections of the liturgy. Teaching to and from the rites is a critical skill, not only for you as a catechetical leader, but also for your baptismal preparation team that you will train on this. Without this skill, the liturgy may feel clunky or disintegrated, almost like an "add on" to your catechetical work. *With* this skill, your catechesis will pour forth from and harmonize with the liturgy, giving the opportunity for faith and reason to integrate and the liturgy to come alive and be personal, allowing that connection between faith and living the faith.

> *The liturgy is one of the essential and indispensable sources of the Church's catechesis, not only because catechesis is able to draw its contents, vocabulary, actions, and words of faith from the liturgy, but above all because the two belong to one another in the very act of believing . . . Liturgy and catechesis are inseparable and nourish one another.* [71]

The Bare Minimum: Essential, Canonical Requirements for Baptism

Anytime we study the Church's teachings, it's important to remember that — at its heart — sacramental preparation is not just informational, but also formational and transformational. We do not learn catechetical things simply so we can know them. We also learn those things so we can live them. There is an ancient Latin saying: *lex orandi, lex credendi, lex vivendi,* which means how we pray forms what we believe, which forms how we live.

Even though we are catechetical leaders, we are not immune from unintentionally stumbling into a few different "landmines" on the spiritual battlefield. If we are catechists at heart, one liability is erring toward a program that is one-sidedly cognitive or academic. Our own enthusiasm or our own discouragement (especially if we've worked with parents who are nominally

Catholic) can lead us to require more than is truly required, insisting that parents complete a variety of additional tasks, before they can have their child baptized. Perhaps, we ask parents to attend a series of two-hour classes, or be a registered, tithing member of our parish for at least six months? These are well-intentioned objectives and very good things in and of themselves, but they are not valid requisites for Baptism. The *Directory for Catechesis* urges us to remember that an encounter with Christ, ". . . does not concern only the mind, but also the body and above all the heart." [72] Laying on too heavy of a burden may trample the tiny seed of faith that brought parents to us in the first place.

In contrast, if we are deeply pastoral and compassionate, but avoid formation, another liability may be neglecting the task of fostering knowledge in catechesis, focusing on the lived human experience and integration into the community, but not awakening and attending to a family's spiritual needs. Perhaps, we know that parents are seeking Baptism for inadequate reasons, or have serious objections to the Catholic faith, but we gloss over these obstacles and accept watered-down consent instead of the beginnings of conversion. The *Directory for Catechesis* also exhorts us ". . . not to underestimate this cognitive dimension of the faith, and to be attentive to integrating it into the educational process of integral Christian maturation." [73] If we fail to do so, we leave their tiny seed of faith out in the sun, before allowing it to develop the deep roots that would keep it from wilting, shriveling up, or being carried away by the first wind that blows.

> *A catechesis, in fact, that sets up an opposition between the content and the experience of faith would show itself to be worthless. Without the experience of faith one would be deprived of a true encounter with God and with one's brothers; the absence of content would block the maturation of faith, keeping one from finding meaning in the Church and living the encounter and exchange with others.* [74]

So, what *is* truly required from a parent who wants their child baptized?

First, desire. They must ask for it. They must truly want Baptism (and not something else that may look similar to it) for their child, like all parents want all good things for their children. "Christian parents will recognize that this practice also accords with their role as nurturers of the life that God has entrusted to them." [75] At the very least, they must not object, permitting instruction of the child in the baptismal faith.

Second, hope. Founded hope that the child will be raised in the Catholic faith. This can be accomplished in a variety of ways through a variety of people. We easily assume this must mean the parents, but nowhere does the Church mandate that the parents must be the source of this founded hope. If they are not up to the responsibility, they can seek support. The godparents in their word and example, the community of the faithful in their help and provision, and the neighbor down the street with her Rosary can all provide this founded hope.

Yes, this hope must be "serious," but it only needs to be seriously the size of a mustard seed. If we start to get into the habit of piling on more than is necessary, we will be guilty of putting ourselves between Christ and the little children He is calling to Himself, sowing seed into thorns, where it will be strangled.[76] On the other hand, if we ignore the call to growth and understanding, we scatter seed on the path, where it will likely be snatched away by the evil one. An accompanying catechesis knows that conversion lies in the tension. After all, "[t]he faith required for Baptism is not a perfect and mature faith, but a beginning that is called to develop . . . 'What do you ask of God's Church?' The response is: 'Faith!'" [77]

Aren't there times when we *should* refuse or delay Baptism for proper reasons?

Yes, there are. They are rare, but they do exist. In these situations, Part Two of the magisterial document *Instruction on Infant Baptism (Pastoralis actio)* offers us two governing principles, "... the second of which is subordinate to the first." [78]

1. Baptism, which is necessary for salvation, is the sign and the means of God's prevenient grace, which frees us from original sin and communicates to us a share in divine life. (By prevenient grace, we mean that grace precedes, anticipates, or comes before human action). Considered in itself, the gift of these blessings to infants must not be delayed.

2. Assurances must be given that the gift, thus granted, can grow by an authentic education in the faith and Christian life, in order to fulfill the true meaning of the sacrament. As a rule, these assurances are to be given by the parents or close relatives, although various substitutions are possible within the Christian community. But if these assurances are not really serious there can be grounds for delaying the sacrament; and if they are certainly nonexistent, the sacrament should even be refused.

How do you know if these assurances are not really serious? This becomes a question of individual discernment that is entrusted to the pastor. If he is to err, he is generally to err on the side of administering the sacrament. To answer this question more thoroughly, refer to (the very brief) Part Two "Answers to Difficulties Being Raised Today" of *Pastoralis actio*.

FIELD NOTES—with Margaret Wickware

"I can remember going into baptismal preparation sessions with 16 pages of notes thinking, 'I have this catechetical mandate, I have to give these parents everything I know about Baptism in an hour and a half to equip them.' I thought the key was to help parents understand their role and share in their own Baptism, you know, the threefold role as priest, prophet, king. I thought this was going to be a revelation to these parents. I did get some say 'Oh, that's really interesting,' but I don't think it was enough. I've had a room full of 25 parents who don't say anything. I talk for two hours and they fill the requirement.

I now realize that we have to look closely at *who* we're talking to and *listen* closely to what they're saying. The 'meat' of the sacrament is going to be like the seed in the parable of the sower. It's clear to me that we need to have rich soil, before we can give them the meat of catechesis. I was trying to give them all meat, and you know, they were only ready for mother's milk. Now, I start talking about *them*, about the culture they're living in, asking how they want to raise their child in the face of this culture, and asking how we can help them. It's more like the evangelization and precatechumenate portion of the OCIA, this beginning stage of Baptism preparation. It's a journey, like Christ on the road to Emmaus. It takes time." [79]

Step Four

The Upstream Opportunity

> *Happy is our sacrament of water, in that, by washing away the sins of our early blindness, we are set free and admitted into eternal life . . . [W]e, little fishes after the example of our [Great] Fish, Jesus Christ, are born in water, nor have we safety in any other way than by permanently abiding in water.* [80]

∽

IMAGINE YOU AND A FRIEND ARE LEISURELY STROLLING ALONG the bank of a river, enjoying a cool, autumn afternoon, while you take in the scenery. You pause at something floating in the water, then squint to see clearly. Suddenly, you realize the floating object is a *child*. And he's in trouble. Without hesitation, you rip off your jacket and jump into the water to pull him to safety. After helping him onto shore, you collapse and catch your breath. Immediately, your friend starts screaming, "There's another one! Another kid in the river!" You turn like lightning as a rush of adrenaline hits your system. Mustering a second wind, you dive back into the water — quickly swimming out to rescue a little girl, just in the nick of time. Wrapping your arms around her, you kick toward the riverbank, coughing and sputtering, as you reach the warm sand.

By now you feel the chill of water in your bones. You stumble for your jacket, but instead hear your friend crying your name. Again. You freeze. You don't know if you have the strength to do this a third time. But what choice do you have? As you struggle to pull yet another drowning victim from the waters, you notice your friend abruptly turn away and start walking upstream. "Wait!" you shout in disbelief, "Where are you going? You're leaving me to rescue these kids by myself?" Resolved, your friend shouts back, "I'm not leaving! I'm going to find out why they are falling in the river in the first place!"

Credited to many originating sources, this tale (often called the "River Story" or the "Upstream Parable") is used in a variety of industries to spark discussion about primary prevention.[81] In other words, it reminds us we can easily spend all our time playing lifeguard, but never look for the *root cause* of the problem, which could eliminate the need to pull kids from the river altogether. So, why tell you this parable? What does it have to do with infant baptismal preparation? If we may speak frankly, the fact that you picked up this book means you suspect there's at least *something* in need of reform or recalibration in your own ministerial work. Applying the principle of primary prevention means we walk "upstream" to take a closer look at *our first and most critical point* of contact with a family: *Baptism*.

Although we can't transform the larger culture (at least not overnight), we do possess a great deal of control over our own parish pulse. What we do (or don't do) in this moment of baptismal preparation sets the tone for *everything* that comes afterward. If we're seeing problems "downstream" (Mass attendance, disengaged students, decreasing sacraments, and so on), it's very probable that there's an "upstream" cause. Thus, the significance of this first Sacrament of Initiation demands that we properly identify the needs of our people, both objectively (in catechesis and doctrine), as well as subjectively (in felt, human needs). Think of how Jesus often healed physical ailments *and* revealed spiritual truth simultaneously. The human and the divine are necessary for fruitful incarnational ministry. This chapter will help with both. If you've ever felt like you're "going back into the river" one too many times, allow us to grab your hand, wrap you in a warm towel, and take you upstream to find a better way.

❧ Task: Your Customized Parish Inventory ❧

The Catholic Church is universal — we share the same call, Creed, and commission. But the Catholic Church is also diverse, in its unique local strengths and its particular regional challenges. Modern struggles in ministry vary, from drastic decline in numbers to fractures in family structures to large scale poverty and persecution. Although global statistics can be helpful, the most critical data will come from closely assessing the doctrinal and ministerial needs of *your* people in *your* parish. Evaluation of your ministerial efforts may not be something you've previously considered, or it may have been limited to a singular data point like "how many children were baptized in any given year?" Although that's an excellent place to start, with your hope for baptismal preparation that is as fruitful as it is valid, we'll have to dig a bit deeper.

This next task is a *three-part inventory* to help you accurately complete a self-assessment of your own parish's current baptismal preparation process. It will take you a bit of time to accomplish. There are quite a few questions to work through, and although they are all taken from the Church's hopes for this area of ministry, many of them may have never crossed your mind before. But don't panic. We don't expect that you'll have a great answer — or even any answer — for some of these questions. In fact, *that's sort of the point.* Don't be afraid to answer with "nothing" or "we don't." What is important is that you answer where you are at this moment with your most honest assessment. We've left these hard questions in as a good and necessary challenge for you — someone who wants to work with the mind and heart of the Church. If we start by asking the right questions, it will be much easier to arrive at the right answers.

If you have priests, deacons, catechists, or volunteers working alongside you, if at all possible, *plan to complete this exercise together*, in person or virtually, if that's easier. The *Directory for Catechesis* strongly encourages catechists to participate not only in program execution, but also in "... the various phases of analysis, planning, selection of materials, implementation, and evaluation."[82] This exercise will be an excellent way to begin or continue your ministerial work with your team. Doing this collaboratively will also relieve some of the burden you may feel as a "lone soldier" in the trenches of ministry. Even if you're the only one officially running infant baptismal preparation, consider inviting one other person (a prayer partner, a volunteer catechist, a deacon, a parent, and so on) to complete this exercise with you.

Consequently, because of the time this exercise will take, and *because of the need to work through it with your team*, it may be a good idea to schedule this task for a later time and set aside this book until then. Trust us, the data it will provide will be worth the wait! After all, how can we tell what we need if we don't know what we have? (If for some reason working together with your team simply isn't possible, you certainly have our permission to keep moving, as it would be better to do this inventory alone than to skip it altogether!)

Whenever you complete your inventory, remember that you don't need to do anything about the data, yet. Right now, you're just "testing the soil." Whether your results end up being dismal or dynamite . . . be not afraid!

Parish Inventory Exercise

Part 1: Your Parish's Baptismal Records

Begin by locating your parish's sacramental records. If you can't access physical records, find a spreadsheet or database containing Baptism data. Look for the babies baptized 20 years ago, 15 years ago, 10 years ago, 5 years ago, and last year. Allowing margin for those who've moved away, how many of these children (and families) are still at your parish? Of those still here, what percentage is actively engaged in the life of the parish (By "active" we mean regularly attending Mass, receiving the Sacrament of Reconciliation, and engaging in some sort of ministry effort, serving or being served). You don't need to be incredibly precise. Make your best guesses. If you're newer to the parish, ask longtime parishioners if they know these families. Use the column below to record your data:

	Number Baptized	Number Still at Parish	Number Still Actively Engaged in the Faith*
20 Years Ago			
15 Years Ago			
10 Years Ago			
5 Years Ago			
1 Year Ago			

*Because we're trying to gauge active participation in faith in connection to your baptismal preparation process, this number certainly may include active families who've recently moved away. We'll leave that choice up to you.

Part 2: Your Parish's Baptism Preparation

Describe your current offerings to families *before* Baptism (feel free to include additional information not indicated by the prompts):

Doctrinal Components:

- What must be completed before a family has their child baptized? How long does it take?

- What curriculum or program do you use? How do you administer it? What is covered?

- How do you assess the parents' understanding of and consent to the essential content?

- How does your process help parents understand and participate in the Sunday liturgy?

- What portion of your preparation involves and/or catechizes the child's godparents?

Ministerial Components:

- How do you meet the needs of expecting and new parents within your parish community?

- In what concrete ways does your community build trust with parents before baby is born?

- Who, from the parish, will the parents meet during their preparation time?

- Is there any difference in preparation for a family baptizing their first baby versus a family baptizing second, third, or subsequent children? If so, what?

Part 3: Your Parish's Post-Baptismal Formation

Describe your current offerings to families *after* Baptism (feel free to include additional information not indicated by the prompts):

Doctrinal Components:

- Do you have a process for moving parents from preparation (teaching *to* the rite) to deeper catechetical formation (teaching *from* the rite)? If so, describe.

- How do you awaken, equip, and encourage parents in their vocation?

- What formation do you provide for adults who want to grow in their Catholic faith?

- How do you help parents enter into the Sunday liturgy more deeply?

- What catechetical "tethers" help families stay connected to your parish between Baptism and their next formal catechetical point of contact, for example sacramental prep?

Ministerial Components:

- How are young families tenderly accompanied into the community of your parish?

- How do you meet the needs (physical, emotional, spiritual) of new mothers?

- How do you meet the needs (physical, emotional, spiritual) of new fathers?

- Do you offer any practical marriage or parenting support, for example, counseling?

- What programs or outreach specifically minister to parents and children ages 0–5?

- Do you have any special spaces in your parish designed for young children?

- Do you offer any kind of childcare or special children's programming for children 0–5?

- How do you connect families with children 0–5 to other families in the same stage?

Anything else you wish to share about your parish's pre- or post-baptismal process? If so, jot it down in the space below.

Ready for a breather? That task required some heavy lifting, and you should be pleased with the work it took to see it through. This task is worth every bit of effort and its results will be incredibly helpful to you in the chapters ahead. For now, set aside the data from this inventory (rest assured, we'll come back to it and put it to good use in your planning efforts) and go take a well-deserved break. Stretch, meander outside, grab a cup of tea or coffee . . . whatever fills your cup (literally or metaphorically). Before you do, take just a moment to pray for those who've been baptized in your parish during the last two decades, regardless of where they are now. Ask the Holy Spirit to hover over the waters once again and stir up the baptismal graces poured into their soul.

The Principle of the Thing

After that inventory, you might be ready to make some changes. But before you grab a sledgehammer and start renovating, remember that in parish ministry, as in other areas of life, it's easy for us to confuse principles with practices. We can see a fancy program or helpful curriculum that seems to work wonders for the parish next door, then jump at the chance to do it ourselves. *Or* we can watch the same program or curriculum completely tank, then dismiss it all and decide we'll never touch that with a ten-foot pole. All this back-and-forth can leave a parish catechetical leader constantly chasing down the next new thing, while simultaneously wondering why all their nets are coming up empty. Understanding the principle behind a practice helps you understand *why* something works or doesn't work, therefore giving you the guidance you need to select practices *that apply to your specific situation best*, yet still honor the universal principles.

A *principle* is something essentially unchanging and universally applicable. For example, a principle in the area of weight loss would be, "You must be in a calorie deficit, in order to lose weight." In most areas of life, there are only a handful of true principles. A *practice* takes a principle and turns it into an implementable action. For example, "Log your daily calorie intake," "Drink more water," "Try intermittent fasting," "Lift weights," "Eat more protein and less refined sugar," "Use smaller plates," "Walk every day," and so on. Practices are often a dime a dozen, so it's important to choose the ones that fit your specific situation, abilities, and commitment level. It's also critical that we don't implement unhealthy or damaging practices (for example "don't eat anything but celery" will definitely put you into a calorie deficit, but at grave [and bland] expense).

With that in mind, let's turn to three universal principles from the *Directory for Catechesis* that can be applied to infant baptismal preparation at every parish and in every place:

Three Principles for Infant Baptism Preparation

1. See your "student" as the whole family

Although we are baptizing infants, our ministry efforts must target the whole family — in this moment, primarily the parents. After all, infants aren't choosing to spend their Sundays at home instead of going to Mass. They don't prefer to watch sports, or take a trip out of town, or any other number of activities that draw them away from the Church. This is why "*[t]he Church proclaims the Gospel to the family.*" [83] We must minister to parents if we desire that they and their child develop a vibrant faith life. Attending to the entire family fixes the gap instead of propagating the cycle. Hence, the *Directory for Catechesis* puts heavy emphasis on ministry to and evangelization of families, and not simply on catechetical programming.

New parents are in a time of massive upheaval (the addition of any child, but particularly the first, is a time of significant change). They are excited. They are scared. They are ecstatic. They are neurotic. They have a plan. They are crippled by self-doubt. To top it off, there are few (if any) reprieves for stepping away and catching their breath to gain perspective on their new situation. Modern and often unnatural social structures remove them from community and support. They've welcomed the most complex creature in the universe with only nine months to prepare and no operating manual and plenty of advice from everyone.

In this time, we need to follow in the way of the great Teacher, Who healed the sick, fed the hungry, grieved with the mourning, and celebrated with the joyful. We need to be involved enough with the parents, individually and communally, to help heal their wounds and feed their hunger — not just now at this moment of Baptism preparation, but in the years, months, weeks, and long (sleepless) nights to come. When we make an effort to welcome, listen to, and understand the reason why parents come to have their children baptized, we "provide an appropriate pathway for them to reawaken the grace of the gift of faith that they have received." [84] We prioritize them not only to reach their child, but also for their own sake. They are parents, yes, but they never cease to be sons and daughters of God.

FIELD NOTES—with Dr. Joseph White

> "Years ago, the United States Conference of Catholic Bishops commissioned a study looking at parents' willingness to engage in sacramental preparation and how it varied sacrament by sacrament. They found one sacrament where parents were willing to do much *more* than most catechetical leaders were expecting of them: *Baptism*. Why? Because when you have a child (especially your first), a *lot* of things change in your life — the routines you have, the sleep you get, the finances you manage, the people you hang out with, the order of your priorities, and so on. When you're bringing home an infant, you're looking in the back seat going, 'We have this soul to be responsible for! It all depends on us. We've got to provide for the needs of this person — physical, spiritual, financial, and so on.' For many parents, that feels overwhelming, at least initially. During this period of family restructuring, parents *want* more connectedness and community than ever before."

2. Infuse your baptismal preparation with the *kerygma* (the Good News!).

Kerygma is the buzzword of our time, so chances are you may have already grown tired of hearing it, even if you may not really understand what it means. Though it may seem novel, the *kerygma* is nothing new — not a papal initiative, Protestant invention, or an oversight of the Apostolic Fathers. It is simply the core of our Catholic faith. It is the story of how God took on our humanity, so that our humanity may participate in God.[85] It is the Good News: "Jesus Christ loves you; He gave His life to save you; and now He is living at your side every day to enlighten, strengthen, and free you." [86] The reason that it's become so popular lately is only because we we realized we had started taking it for granted, assuming people had heard its message and responded to it affirmatively.

The *Directory for Catechesis* explicitly points out the intimate relationship between *kerygma* and catechesis.[87] Think of the catechetical elements of our faith — all the topics we know, love, and love to teach — like the pieces of a puzzle. The *kerygma* is like the picture on the cover of the box for that puzzle. It pulls everything together. It makes everything make sense. Without it, we have a bunch of random pieces. With it, we have a vision, a picture, a story. *Evangelii gaudium* reminds us to never ". . . assume that our audience . . . is capable of relating what we say to the very heart of the Gospel." [88] In the ancient Church, because Baptism was often a likely path to martyrdom, it would be unlikely to meet a baptized Christian who had not wholeheartedly understood and believed the Good News of Jesus Christ. That's why the catechumenate (now Order of Christian Initiation for Adults (OCIA), was the Rite of Christian Initiation for Adults (RCIA)) lasted years before initiating a person into the sacred mysteries.

Unfortunately, in many parts of the world today, ". . . an administrative approach prevails over a pastoral approach, as does a concentration on administering the sacraments apart from other forms of evangelization." [89] So, even if a person has been baptized (it doesn't matter if it's a parent, a parish catechetical leader, or a priest), he or she may never have heard the Gospel proclaimed in a way that is deeply personal, incarnate, and relevant. (How can people know, if no one told them?[90]) Even more importantly, he or she may have never been given the chance to personally *respond* to that proclamation — the invitation of the Bridegroom proposing an eternal life together. (Though He deeply desires our "yes," He will always wait for our consent). For many within our parishes, this response cannot be taken for granted. In other words, "although they have already received the gift of baptismal grace, [they] do not actually taste its richness." [91]

FIELD NOTES—with Dr. Joseph White

"In baptismal preparation, more than any other sacrament, we work with people who are only marginally connected with the parish. That makes Baptism a really important evangelization opportunity that needs to begin with the *kerygma* — why we want to be baptized in the first place. We begin with this aim to evangelize parents, not just inform them. Give them a meaningful encounter with Jesus Christ. In her book *Forming Intentional Disciples: The Path to Knowing and Following Jesus*, Sherry Weddell talks about the difference between someone who's an intentional disciple, and somebody who is kind of connected to the parish — maybe they even come every Sunday, but they're not an intentional disciple. The difference is that an intentional disciple can point back to a time, when they had a meaningful encounter with Jesus that transformed their life. It's the experience of the *kerygma* that helps us identify as disciples of Jesus and not just people who go to church."

3. Accompany families *through* Baptism, not just *to* Baptism.

American geneticist Dean Hamer once tried to figure out why brain scans of those who are very religious literally look different from those who don't practice religion at all. As a geneticist, Hamer assumed there must be a gene, calling it the "God gene." Eventually, scientists discovered that genes were responsible for very little in this structural difference, instead concluding that individuals whose brains appear "more religious" had been exposed and "attached" to their faith at a very young age in life.[92] This makes sense. Developmentally, we know that the part of the brain most responsible for relationship to parents is *prime* in the first six years of life, often referred to as "the window of attachment." In this window we learn (not explicitly but in the wiring of our brain), what safe, loving relationships feel like (or at least, that's the goal). As the brain ages and becomes less malleable, attachment becomes a more difficult and complicated process.

What does brain science have to do with those of us in catechesis? A great deal, believe it or not, especially if we work in baptismal preparation.

These critical early years (0–6, but particularly 0–3) are a golden opportunity for "attaching" children to Christ and His Church (something done primarily through their parents). When journeying with parents requesting Baptism for their child, the *Directory for Catechesis* exhorts us ". . . to provide adequate time for it to unfold," [93] using words like "ongoing," "gradual" and "progressive" to describe the process of conversion.[94] With the right kind of accompaniment for a family, how many thousands of mealtime or bedtime prayers, conversations about faith, visits to the church, sacred images around the house, and blessings from the priest could be had in these early years? This kind of formation ". . . in the living womb of the Christian community, helps the baptized person to *take shape* . . ." [95]

Without that type of accompaniment and motherly care, families are often left alone during these golden years after Baptism. In fact, the next "formal" point of catechesis offered is often the Sacraments of Reconciliation and Eucharist some seven years later. A lot can (or may not) happen in seven years! Accompanying families *through* Baptism means we begin to prioritize the five to six years of post-baptismal catechumenate *at least as* much as we prioritize pre-baptismal preparation (you might say it's an "upstream" idea). By doing so, "[t]he Church, patiently accompanying Her children and respecting the pace of their maturing, shows Herself to be an attentive Mother." [96] Just imagine how vibrant our parish communities might look if we invested a great deal of time building trust, cultivating intimacy, and nurturing the communal relationship with the newly baptized and their families, not just in this one moment, but in the millions of moments that follow.

FIELD NOTES—with Dr. Joseph White

"I think the problem is not that we give the parents too much, but that we don't give them enough. Years ago, there was another study looking at why parents were overscheduling their kids — psychologists raised the alarm and social scientists asked, 'if parents are so stressed out, why are they doing it [overscheduling]?' They thought maybe parents felt pressure to have their kids involved in several activities. Once they dug underneath the surface, they found that people, even subconsciously, were looking for community and connection. Parents were putting kids in activities — preschool, ballet, gymnastics, soccer, and so on — partly to meet their own need for community. During this time, do we as a parish say to parents, 'We'll fit you right in, we'll help you get connected to people!?' No, far more often we say 'Okay, come back in seven years!' Then, by the time the child is school age or in religious education, the parents respond, 'But how can we do more, don't you see all the other things we're doing right now?' And remember that whatever they choose to do or get involved in for their first child, they will likely repeat for any future children. That's why this moment of Baptism is so important. It sets the tone."

Conclusion

Just as a new baby can be overwhelming for parents, a baptismal preparation ministry can be overwhelming for catechetical leaders. It's easy to get lost in the circuit of curriculum and conferences, doing your best but always feeling a bit like you're failing. This chapter may have opened your eyes to new questions (many perhaps without answers), not because we want to further overwhelm you, but because we want to help you cut through the noise and prioritize the *most* important things. The exercises we've given you in each chapter have already been equipping you with critical, principle-based skills that will help you confidently make the right decisions and take the next steps for a vibrant, fruitful baptismal preparation process in your parish.

It won't happen overnight. But it's not supposed to. The birth of a baptismal preparation process (like the birth of a baby) is a beginning. A tiny seed. It is a slow, beautiful process of growth and transformation, not only guided by the Holy Spirit, but also nurtured by your own hands. Need we remind you that the Lord entrusted this particular parish to *you* — not to the catechetical leader down the road or across town. *You* have been called to this place, at this time. *You* are the one the Lord wants to labor with, as you birth new souls into the Kingdom of Heaven. Whether you feel like it or not, *you* are the right person for this job. As we move into the next section of this book, it's finally time to plan some of the more practical pieces of your baptismal preparation process. But what kind of guide would we be if we asked you to accompany families at Baptism and beyond, but then *we* didn't accompany you? As has been the case with this entire book thus far, you don't have to do this next part alone!

> ## Really, You're Not Alone!
>
> We're happy to be your cheerleaders, as you work through this book, but we're not the only ones here to support you. Here are a few suggestions for finding guidance and solidarity closer to home:
>
> - **Reach out to another parish.** Are there nearby parishes that have exceptional ministries in this area of infant baptismal preparation? Consider taking a "field trip!" Reach out to their priest or program coordinator and ask if you could visit and discuss their process over coffee. It can be so helpful to connect with a fellow "soldier in the trenches," especially one who lives close to you. You might walk away with some new ideas or even a new friend.
>
> - **Reach out to your diocese.** Are there diocesan resources available for this area of infant baptismal preparation? Those who work within your local diocese are often thrilled to help support, coach, and encourage you. They can guide you toward resources you may not be aware of, connect you to other parish catechetical leaders, and offer you an empathic ear! They may even be willing to mentor you personally in this area.
>
> **Reach out to the *Catechetical Institute* at Franciscan University of Steubenville.** One of the best parts of the *Catechetical Institute* is its commitment to "Forming those who form others." Through this platform, you can request an individual mentor (usually someone else also in the trenches of parish ministry) to walk you through the *Catechetical Institute's* workshops on Franciscan At Home (FrancsicanAtHome.com) or you can join the *International Guild for Catechists and Leaders* (FrancsicanAtHome.com/guild). Either option will connect you with other catechetical leaders across the globe, either for guidance or solidarity and collaboration!

Step Five

Program Planning: Master Planning Worksheet

Dear friends! To you I entrust the task of making a decisive contribution to the evangelization of your country. Take Christ into the Third Millennium. Trust Him! His promise spans the centuries: 'Whoever loses his life for my sake and the Gospel's will save it' (Mark 8:35). Do not be afraid! Life with Christ is a wonderful adventure.[97]

∽

Though we're nearing the end of this book, the adventure of program planning is just beginning — a process you will likely repeat again and again, as you progress in your ministerial task. Your work in the previous chapters has built a foundation to help you enter this phase with proper posture and skill. That's why this next chapter is essentially one big task — a master planning worksheet that will guide you in sketching out the right baptismal preparation process for you. Whether you're starting from scratch or fine-tuning an existing program, this worksheet will help you take our universal principles and extract the specific practices and next right steps — customized to your parish, considerate of your resources, and curated by the Holy Spirit!

Like a choose-your-own-adventure book,[98] this planning worksheet will also point you toward specific, "*a la carte*" chapters toward the end of this book, as well as any external resources that we think could be valuable in your particular circumstances. You are welcome to read all of these chapters or focus only on the specific ones that relate to your current needs. You may duplicate this worksheet and use it as many times as you like, now and in the years to come. As with the customized parish inventory from the previous chapter, plan to complete this master planning worksheet *with* your team, even if it's small.

We hope you're beginning to believe that transformation and great fruitfulness is possible in your own parish. But we also know you may start to feel that the task ahead is too great (not only in this book, but also in infant baptismal preparation as a whole). "What's wrong with offering one brief prep session?" you might say. "If we ask for more, won't families shop around for an easier requirement? If we offer more, won't our volunteers want to quit?" We certainly know what it's like to stare at the mountain in front of you and feel the urge to turn around and go home. "Let's just keep it short and simple, so we don't lose people."

But the reality is that this approach typically *does* lose people. If not now, then years down the road. Saint John Paul II's motto for the Third Millenium was taken from the *Gospel of Luke:* "*Put out into the deep.*" [99] He wrote, ". . . [I]t would be wrong to think that ordinary Christians can be content with a shallow prayer that is unable to fill their whole life. Especially in the face of the many trials to which today's world subjects faith, they would be not only mediocre Christians, but 'Christians at risk.'" [100] In other words, without fundamentally rethinking how we approach families with the Gospel, those we are baptizing will ultimately grow up to be "Christians at risk."

We know you are often overwhelmed and carrying heavy burdens. But we also trust that you desire to say "yes" to Christ's invitation to "put out in the deep," even when it's not easy. As you embark upon this exercise and navigate the sometimes-stormy waters of catechesis in your own "sea," remember that your choices matter a great deal in the unfolding of salvation history currently taking place in your particular parish. And rest assured, the Holy Spirit will always guide you, as you discern which course to take. With that in mind, let's begin by asking Mary, the Star of the Sea, to guide us safely in our earthly journey, as we aim for Heaven's shore:

In the name of the Father, and of the Son, and of the Holy Spirit. Amen.

Mary, Star of the Sea, light of every ocean,
guide seafarers across all dark and stormy seas
that they may reach the haven of peace and light
prepared in Him Who calmed the sea.
As we set forth upon the oceans of the world
and cross the deserts of our time, show us, O Mary,
the fruit of your womb, for without your Son we are lost.
Pray that we will never fail on life's journey,
that in heart and mind, work and deed,
in days of turmoil and in days of calm,
we will always look to Christ and say,
"Who is this that even wind and sea obey Him?"
Our Lady of Peace, pray for us!
Bright Star of the Sea, guide us!
Our Lady, Star of the Sea, pray for seafarers, pray for us.
Our Lady, Star of the Sea, help and protect us!
Sweet Mother I place this cause in your hands. [101]

Ready to get started? This worksheet contains three sections. They will each take time to work through, but they will be worth it!

To complete Section One, you'll begin by gathering your work from this book into one place, making it easy to access and reference with no needless flipping back and forth between pages. If you are going through this worksheet with a team, have each member complete the first section individually, either at the beginning of your time together, or before you meet. After completing Section One, pause and read the Introduction to Section Two before proceeding.

Section One: Review and Reflect

"Blessed are those who hunger and thirst for righteousness, for they shall be satisfied." [102]

Name of Parish(es):

What type of parish (single, clustered, merged, and so on):

Parish Location:

Take a few moments to reflect:

- What is unique about your parish?

- As a whole, what do you feel is your parish's greatest strength or charism?

- As a whole, what do you feel is your parish's greatest weakness or liability?

- How many families belong to your parish? Of them, how many currently have children under the age of 5 years old?

- How many priests are currently assigned to your parish?

- Do you have any deacons at your parish? If so, how many?

- Currently, how many paid staff members do you have at your parish, if any?

- What is *your* current role within the parish? Are you paid or are you a volunteer? How did you get involved with baptismal preparation ministry?

- Briefly describe the demographic of your parish community (both within the church's congregation and in the surrounding neighborhood).

Think or look back to the exercise titled "The Dream" back in Chapter 1 [page 30]. Below, reiterate four to five summarized points from that exercise. If you had unlimited time and resources, what would the baptismal preparation program of your dreams look like?

Next, taking cue from the exercise titled "Side by Side" in Chapter 2 [page 57], where did *your* dreams for baptismal preparation ministry line up with *God's* dreams? Write down two or three similarities in the space below.

If you need help jogging your memory, these are God's desires for Baptism, as laid out in the *Catechism of the Catholic Church*, specifically paragraph 1213:

1. God desires to free us from sin.

2. God desires to give us new birth as sons and daughters of God.

3. God desires that we are incorporated into His Church, ultimately sharing in Her mission.

In Chapter 3, we looked at the ritual text for the *Order of Baptism of Children*, specifically noting the importance of teaching to and from the rite. Based on this, how well do you feel that your current baptismal preparation process prepares parents and godparents to understand and participate in the baptismal liturgy? Using the columns below, write down each of the sections of the rite, gauging how well you feel your current process addresses these items:

As a reminder, these are the sections of the Rite of Baptism:

- Rite of Receiving the Child
- Sacred Celebration of the Word of God
  - Biblical Readings and Homily
  - Prayer of the Faithful
  - Prayer of Exorcism and Anointing before Baptism
- Celebration of Baptism
  - Blessing of Water and Invocation of God over the Water
  - Renunciation of Sin and Profession of Faith
  - Baptism
- Explanatory Rites
  - Anointing after Baptism
  - Clothing with a White Garment
  - Handing On of a Lighted Candle
  - "Ephphatha"
- Conclusion of the Rite
  - Lord's Prayer
  - Blessing and Dismissal

For Example:

Very Well	Moderately	Poorly
Handing on of a Lighted Candle — We take the time to explain what the light of Christ means to the parents in our preparation process.	Clothing with a White Garment — The child normally begins wearing white, but what if we had the child begin in something else, and then placed the white garment on them during the rite?	Rite of Receiving the Child — We don't explain this at all; parents and godparents probably aren't prepared to understand the significance.

Now it's your turn!

Very Well	Moderately	Poorly

Very Well	Moderately	Poorly

For these next questions, refer to your answers from the customized parish inventory on page 81, as well as the universal principles from the Directory for Catechesis.

In your customized parish inventory, which doctrinal or ministerial components of your current baptismal preparation or post-baptismal process surprised you, in a *good* way? What were some of your greatest strengths or offerings? What are you doing very well?

In your customized parish inventory, which doctrinal or ministerial components of your current baptismal preparation or post-baptismal process seemed lacking? Where do you find that you had the least to offer? What struck you about these areas?

No need to flip back and forth! These are **the three universal principles for infant baptismal preparation,** as laid out in the *Directory for Catechesis*:

- See your "student" as the whole family.[103]

- Infuse your baptismal preparation with the kerygma.[104]

- Accompany families through Baptism, not just to Baptism.[105]

Of the three universal principles from the *Directory*, which one do you feel your current baptismal preparation process does the *best*? Why? How? Reflect and make a few notes below.

Of these three principles, which one do you feel your current baptismal preparation process *struggles* with the most? Why? How? Reflect and make a few notes below.

Before completing this section, is there anything else you'd like to note about your parish, as a whole, or your baptismal preparation program? If so, jot it down in the space below.

Program Planning: Master Planning Worksheet

To complete Section Two, plan to gather your team and make sure you can visit the Blessed Sacrament, and, if possible, have Eucharistic Adoration. Throughout this book, we've reiterated the importance of being docile to the Holy Spirit and seeking God's desires for our parish programs. This exercise is no different! Section Two is a guided meditation, but with more practical planning components, showing Jesus' guidance. Although you will all be with Jesus corporately, each member of your team should complete Section Two silently and individually. This is the first part of a creative process called "brainwriting," an approach different from what we know as "brainstorming." Since the best ideas are often born in moments of quiet, this exercise asks each member of the team to be individually inspired by the Holy Spirit, listening for His guidance and exercising their own creativity, as they write down their thoughts, plans, and ideas.

Just as a heads up, later on in this worksheet (Section Three) all members of the team will gather to share and prune their ideas together, noticing similarities and discerning the Holy Spirit's invitation for which steps to take next.

Section Two: Invite the Inspiration of the Holy Spirit

*"I am the vine, you are the branches.
He who abides in me, and I in him,
he it is that bears much fruit,
for apart from me you can do nothing."* [106]

Welcome back! This second section should be completed in front of the Blessed Sacrament, and if possible, in Eucharistic Adoration. Bring this book and a pen. Plan to spend at least 30–45 minutes with this section. Once you have settled your body, take a few minutes to simply be with Jesus. Notice any thoughts or anxieties that may be on your heart. Bring them to the Lord. Share anything else you want Him to know. When you are ready, move through each of the prompts and questions below. Take your time. Allow the Holy Spirit to lead you. As you answer the questions, take notes of what the Holy Spirit brings to your mind and be prepared to share these thoughts with your team.

Prayer of Invitation to the Holy Spirit

Come, Holy Spirit, fill the hearts of your faithful
and kindle in them the fire of your love.

Send forth your Spirit and they shall be created,
and you shall renew the face of the Earth.

Let us pray.
O God, Who have taught the hearts of the faithful
by the light of the Holy Spirit,
grant that in the same Spirit we may be truly wise
and ever rejoice in his consolation.
Through Christ our Lord. Amen.

As you move through each of the following prompts, take your time. Sit with the Holy Spirit and allow Him to lead you. Don't pressure yourself to move on until He guides you to do so.

Begin this section by inviting the Holy Spirit's consolation. Ask: *Where does our baptismal preparation program converge with the Heart of the Trinity? Where has there been spiritual fruit in our program? How have we been docile to the Holy Spirit's leading?* Ask Him to show you any specific examples that may be encouraging or helpful. Use the space below for your notes.

*The Holy Spirit is rightly called the Consoler.
When the touches of the Spirit, enlightening us and
impelling us to act, are well received, they pour into our hearts
not just light and strength, but solace and peace.* [107]

When you are ready, next consider the types of families who typically approach you for Baptism. Think back to their stories and their situations. Ask the Holy Spirit to show you: *What are the most urgent needs or specific struggles of the families approaching our parish? Materially? Emotionally? Spiritually?* Use the space below to write down what comes to mind.

When you are ready, next invite the Holy Spirit's conviction, remembering that His conviction is always gentle and kind, drawing us back toward communion. Ask: *Where is our baptismal preparation program lacking? Is there anything we are doing or not doing that is blocking the Holy Spirit's movement? What opportunities for fruitfulness or deeper conversion are we missing?* Ask Him to show you what He sees. Resist any tendency toward shame. Use the space below for your notes.

After you've completed the first three prompts, spend the rest of your time inviting the Holy Spirit's faithful and creative inspiration. For each of the three universal principles of baptismal preparation, ask the Holy Spirit: *How would you like this principle to look, specifically within our parish? How should we employ the gifts and resources entrusted to us?* Use the spaces below for your notes.

See your "student" as the whole family.

Infuse your baptismal preparation with the *kerygma*.

Accompany families *through* Baptism, not just *to* Baptism.

> *Those who keep their hearts open to holy inspirations are happy! For they will never lack those that they need in order to live intheir state well and devoutly, and to exercise the duties of their profession in a holy way.* [108]

Conclude your time with a simple, heartfelt prayer of gratitude to the Holy Spirit for His light!

Section Three: Build Your Baptismal Preparation Process

To complete Section Three, once you and your team have completed the first two sections, gather together and complete Section Three collectively as a team. Begin with team discussion, asking each person to share the inspirations they received during reflection or prayer. If possible, have one person take notes on a whiteboard or chalkboard, so everyone can see any common threads:

Questions for Team Discussion:

- What stood out to you as strengths of our parish or our program? What consolations or fruit did the Holy Spirit reveal to you?

- What came to mind as weaknesses or opportunities of our parish or program? What did the Holy Spirit show you was lacking or most needed?

- What do you feel are the most important next steps for our parish and program?

Next, allow your team to be *inspired* by the catechumenate (OCIA) in sketching out the structure for your baptismal preparation process. The catechumenate is the *normative* model for *all* conversion. Think of the four catechumenal stages below like a skeleton or framework. As your program continues to evolve and grow, you'll put on muscle and flesh, each time gaining more agility and movement. Use your notes from Sections One and Two to complete Section Three.

> *The catechumenal inspiration of catechesis does not mean reproducing the catechumenate in a servile manner, but taking on its style and its formative dynamism, responding also to the "need for a mystagogical renewal, one which would assume very different forms based on each educational community's discernment."* [109]

As your team fills in the framework below, make sure your process includes at least one practical component in each of the four stages. Depending on where you are at in your planning, you may already have many offerings in each of these stages, or you may have only one or two items total. The most important thing is not the size of your program, but its fruitfulness in providing opportunities for souls to unite with the Father, Son, and Holy Spirit. Regardless of where you begin, the question to ask is always, "Where is the Holy Spirit inviting us to go from here?"

The Period of Evangelization and Precatechumenate.[110]

Families come seeking Baptism with various reasons, questions, doubts, and curiosities. What does our first point of contact look like (a person, a form, and so on)? Who do they meet? How do we demonstrate hospitality? How do we build trust and relationship? What is asked of them in this stage? How do we discover their reasons for wanting Baptism? When and how is the *kerygma* proclaimed? Are they given a chance to respond personally? This is the stage where the seed for conversion is planted.

The Period of the Catechumenate. For families who have received and accepted the Gospel and truly desire Baptism for their child, this period is set aside for deeper catechesis and the chance to respond to God's gestures of love. What does our catechesis look like? Who leads or teaches? Do we use a curriculum of some kind? How often do we gather families to meet? Individually? As a group with other families? What kind of support do we offer in their own parenting and family life? Are the parents married sacramentally in the Church? Would they like to be? Would they like an appointment with Father to talk about the possibility of being married in the Church, so he can answer any questions they might have? Do we help parents know how to notice when God is active in their lives? Are we teaching to the baptismal rite? When do we help parents experience intimacy with God through prayer? How are we introducing and connecting families to our parish community during this time?

The vast majority of the time, parents (if they are Catholic) have never heard that it's important for them to be sacramentally married in the Church. They often think "getting married is getting married," and it doesn't matter where, by who, and so on. This makes sense, especially if they've had no formal religious education since they were children, and that topic would not have covered at an adult depth then, because they weren't adults then! So why would we be surprised that they don't know? What a great privilege to offer the opportunity for more grace.

The Period of the Purification and Enlightenment. Baptism day is drawing near and families begin more prayerful reflection and preparation for the sacrament, both individually and with the parish community. Are we allowing parents to experience deeper communion with God, at their level? Could we minister to their needs in order to do this (for example, childcare, family-centric experiences, and so on)? Have we given them resources to incorporate at home? Could a priest or deacon visit and bless their homes before the Baptism? Could a lay person bring them a meal and visit with them? Is it possible for parents to receive the Sacrament of Reconciliation before their child's Baptism?

Baptism + Mystagogy. The day of Baptism has come! But the unfolding of these sacred mysteries in the lives of families is just beginning. How can we minister to the catechetical and pastoral needs of parents and families in the following month? Six months? Year? Two, three, four, five, six years? Are we actively helping them to expand their relationships within the community, formally or organically? How do we walk *with* them through the joys and challenges of raising their child in faith? What opportunities do we offer them in this tender stage?

Now that was a great deal of labor, dear friends in Christ! And like the birth of a baby, it is a beautiful ending and a glorious beginning at all once. After you and your team have completed all three sections of the worksheet, conclude in prayer, thanking the Holy Spirit for His guidance and offering up your own ideas to Him. Make rudimentary plans to begin implementing and delegating the next steps of your process at a pace that feels good and doable. Then, rest and celebrate! Take some time with your team (perhaps a "potluck," family-style dinner) to enjoy the fruits of your labor, as well as some community and fellowship with each other. (We are Catholic after all, so feasting is just as important as preparation!)

Last, but not least, remember that this planning process is not "one and done." Following implementation of any new process, there is always a "troubleshooting" period. There will be things to modify. You may find some things don't "land" with your people the way you had intended. This does <u>not</u> mean you should throw out everything! Quite the opposite. This usually means what you're offering is *very close* to "scratching the itch" of those you serve, with just a few minor tweaks. Come back to this planning worksheet as often as you need, relying on your team and the wisdom of the Holy Spirit to effectively minister to those God has entrusted to you!

> *. . . [T]here is no greater freedom than that of allowing oneself to be guided by the Holy Spirit, renouncing the attempt to plan and control everything to the last detail, and instead letting Him enlighten, guide and direct us, leading us wherever He wills. The Holy Spirit knows well what is needed in every time and place.* [111]

Step Six

Choose-Your-Own-Adventure Chapters

~

As you moved through the Master Planning Worksheet, you may have noticed some areas where additional guidance or resources would be helpful for you and your team. The additional chapters in the next part of this book are brief, but laser-focused on these specific areas. Feel free to access the following chapters, as needed:

If you'd like more help with the Period of Evangelization and Precatechumenate:

- The Good News: How to Keep Catechesis Kerygmatic [page 138]

- The Team: Finding and Forming Catechists [page 146]

- The Need: Skills for Building Lasting Relationships with Families [page 156]

- The Parents: Meeting the Unique Needs of Mothers and Fathers [page 172]

If you'd like more help with the Catechumenate:

- The Good News: How to Keep Catechesis *Kerygmatic* [page 138]
- The Team: Finding and Forming Catechists [page 146]
- The Co-Laborers: Working With Godparents [page 166]
- The Village: Involving Your Parish Community in Baptism Preparation [page 192]
- Helpful Tools, Programs, and Resources [page 220]
- The Need: Skills for Building Lasting Relationships with Families [page 156]
- The Parents: Meeting the Unique Needs of Mothers and Fathers [page 172]

If you'd like more help with the period of Purification & Enlightenment:

- The Holy Family: Helping Parents of Young Children Enter into Deeper Prayer [page 180]
- The Village: Involving Your Parish Community in Baptism Preparation [page 192]

If you'd like more help with Mystagogy and post-baptismal formation:

- The Window of Opportunity: Ministering to Families with Children Under 6 [page 186]
- The Village: Involving your Parish Community in Baptism Preparation [page 192]
- Helpful Tools, Programs, and Resources [page 220]

If you have a question that hasn't been answered yet:

- The Exceptions to the Rule: Ministering in Special Situations [page 196]

When parents come to us seeking Baptism for their children, it may look like they have brought nothing to the table, but that's not quite true. They brought their hope. Their greatest work. Their child.

They thirst.

Literally, for Baptism.

Spiritually, for something more than they can even articulate.

Jesus thirsts for them; in fact, their thirst comes from His thirst.

Imagine a baptismal preparation process so meaningful and profound that they don't want to leave after their baby is baptized, but instead find themselves wanting to come back.

Again.

And again.

And again.

Baptism is like birth. New life. It changes everything.

And yet, it is also so small.

A seed.

A start.

The same is true for your baptismal preparation process. The Holy Spirit always seeks to fill our hearts with more of God's love, but in the beginning, He does not ask for much. In His great gentleness, He gives us time to make room and prepare for what He desires to bring in greater measure. Like a woman's body stretches to accommodate new life growing inside of her, we — as the Body of Christ — engage in a similar receptive and stretching work, when we allow the Holy Spirit to bring new life into our parishes. (Even if it involves breathing through a few contractions along the way!)

My children, for whom I am again in labor until Christ be formed in you! [112]

As we embark on this great adventure together, dear friends in Christ, you may want to call the midwife. After all, something beautiful is about to be born.

The Good News:

How to Keep Catechesis *Kerygmatic*

You may (or may not) have heard the word "*kerygma*" used recently — it's been making a comeback in Catholic culture. But what is it? If it sounds Greek to you, you are right. *Kerygma* comes from the Greek meaning, "proclaim" or "herald." That's exactly what we, as catechists, should be doing — proclaiming and heralding. *What* exactly should we be proclaiming and heralding? Simply put, *Jesus* — the Gospel message or the "Good News" of Christ.

The *kerygma* refers to, in more specific terms, what Saint John Paul II called, "... the initial, ardent proclamation, by which a person is one day overwhelmed and brought to the decision to entrust himself to Jesus Christ by faith..." [113] It should always be on our mind, heart, and lips. It should precede any deeper catechesis, as it is very difficult to move forward without the person in front of you having heard and responded to it. It will be the spring from which all the life of faith flows, as well as the ocean it returns to.

How do we do this?

Provided the essentials are present (we proclaim the necessary elements for salvation, we do it in a way that's comfortable for us, and we share a small piece of our personal journey with Jesus), the *kerygma* can be presented in numerous creative ways. Let's look at the essentials in the list below:

- God created humanity — and you — in His own image, with a beautiful plan in mind, for your own benefit and abundant joy. To live forever with Him.

- Humanity — and each one of us — has sinned, by not trusting, by rejecting God, His plan, and His divine life. This has brought brokenness, disorder, suffering, loneliness, and death into our lives.

- In our sinfulness, none of us can atone for the offense against our eternal God and repair the damage we've caused within our own souls.

- As an act of grace, Jesus — the eternally-begotten, divine Son of God — came down from Heaven and united with humanity in the womb of the Virgin Mary. Jesus, then, showed us how to perfectly be united to the Father by His own prayer, teaching, life, suffering, and death on the cross — never once rejecting the Father's love and plan for humanity.

- The power of Jesus' perfect love and obedience conquered death through His Resurrection. By the gift of the Holy Spirit, He offers this same power over death in the promise of eternal life to all who wish to be reunited to the Father.

- He calls you to a new life by accepting His sacrifice as your own, entering into personal relationship with Him, receiving the sacramental life of His Church, and participating in her mission.

- Do you desire this? How will you respond? (Don't forget the invitation and opportunity for their answer).

That's it! There are various versions of this template which have more or fewer steps, but as long as the essentials are present and an invitation is extended, you've proclaimed and heralded the Good News. Feel free to add a very short summary (four to five minutes at most) of how *you* have heard and accepted this Good News and how your own relationship with God continues to impact your life. Don't feel the need to be too specific about any past or present sins. Keep the focus on Jesus and His grace, not personal failings. A good question to speak to is, "How have I fallen in love with Jesus Christ and His Church, and why will this never change (or why will this love only grow deeper)?"

As you share the Good News of Christ, avoid using language that is too elevated for your audience — if you move too fast, you'll overwhelm those you're sharing with. Start with common language they can relate to, then — as they are ready — draw them slowly and intentionally into the richness and beauty of the language of the faith and deeper doctrine, so they can fully savor it. This applies not only in this initial proclamation, or *kerygma,* but also as you move through the specifics of infant Baptism preparation with them.

Last, but not least, take note of this chapter's title: *How to Keep* (not make) *Catechesis Kerygmatic.* This matters because everything the Church has been, is now, and continues to be is *kerygmatic.* The Church ". . . exists in order to evangelize . . ." [114] We're not adding anything novel by keeping our ministry rooted in the Gospel — far from it. Rather, we are drawing strength, power, and efficacy from the Gospel that saves us. If we ever sense that our catechesis is becoming ineffective or falling on deaf ears, we should pause and ask ourselves, "Are we connecting this doctrine we're currently teaching to the *kerygma?*"

> We might want to think about offering a brief, meaningful retreat where those seeking Baptism (perhaps other sacraments, too) can meet and encounter Jesus. At the end of the retreat, each person could be asked to respond personally to Jesus' invitation. Baptism preparation would then begin after someone gave his or her authentic consent. (This also gives people the chance to freely refuse Baptism if entrance into faith is not what they desire.) The Catherine of Sienna Institute's Great Story of Jesus is an example of a *kerygmatic* retreat and can be found here: https://learning.siena.org/product/ananias-who-do-you-say-that-i-am-the-great-story-of-jesus-in-nine-acts/.

In catechesis too, we have rediscovered the fundamental role of the first announcement or kerygma, which needs to be the center of all evangelizing activity and all efforts at Church renewal . . . It is the principal proclamation, the one which we must hear again and again in different ways, the one which we must announce one way or another throughout the process of catechesis, at every level and moment. [115]

❈ Workshop This Chapter ❈

The *kerygma* is not only *the* story. It is *our* story. We are invited into it, not only to proclaim it as a set of truths, but also to participate in it through an intimate relationship with God. It is from this relationship that we can begin to see deeper truths flowing from the *kerygmatic* proclamations.

Want to check and see if your own catechesis is *kerygmatic*? Does your process of baptismal preparation guide souls to the *kerygmatic* truths contained within the doctrines? This exercise will help you put it to the test. Begin by choosing a doctrine, practice, or teaching that is currently part of your baptismal preparation. As the first Sacrament of Initiation, Baptism has many doctrines that naturally lend themselves to being *kerygmatic* — and when working with parents (particularly those who've been away from the Church) other things may also come up, too (not attending Mass, haven't been to the Sacrament of Reconciliation, matters of marriage, and so on). *Everything* can be tied to the *Kerygma*!

Once you've selected your doctrine, practice, or teaching, filter it through the questions below. These questions are not an exact parallel to the points of the proclaimed *kerygma* as written above, but rather a deeper contemplation on our ability to bring people "to the well" [116] of God's infinite love. For whatever doctrine, practice, or teaching you've chosen, write a one or two sentence answer to each of the following:

- How does this doctrine/practice reveal the beauty of God's plan for their life or family?

- How is this doctrine/practice a medicine for sin? How does it fit into God's plan to restore and reconcile the soul?

- How does this doctrine/practice clearly demonstrate God offering more of His infinite love?

- How does this doctrine/practice elevate or speak to the dignity of each as an unrepeatable human person created by God out of love, in His image and likeness?

- How does this doctrine/practice continually transform the human soul?

- What would consistently receiving these graces or engaging in this practice do for this family during the next year, five, ten, or twenty years?

- Is this doctrine/practice something they would like to be a part of? If yes, how could we practically help them embrace this doctrine/practice? What can we do to accompany them and aid them on their spiritual journey?

RESOURCE RECOMMENDATION

There are several workshops on *Franciscan At Home* about the *kerygma* found in the "First Proclamation & Evangelization Track". They are all extremely helpful for further training and practice!

The Team:

Finding and Forming Catechists

Jesus sent His disciples out two by two. Taking notes from the methodology of our Great Catechist, any effort to spread the Good News should be done collectively, whenever possible. From its conception, the Church has always been intended to grow and multiply — not only in membership, but also in leaders, missionaries, and mentors. Which means you now have the privilege of helping others deepen their encounter with Christ, not only those who come to you for baptismal preparation, but also those who come to you to *do* baptismal preparation. Plus, there are perks to doing this as a team:

- ***You benefit.*** Engaging our true mission brings personal satisfaction and joy. You gain teammates who share heartaches and joys with you. You (who probably already have too much to do in too little time) get to distribute the workload, leaving you free to do things *only* you can do (especially if you are a priest). And you reawaken your own excitement for knowledge by catechizing your team at a higher level, sharing deeper truths of the sacrament with those ready and able to receive it.

- ***Your catechists benefit.*** They gain the joy of deeper catechesis and conversion under your guidance, enriching their own love of the Gospel by watching how others come to deeper relationships with Jesus in their care. Empowering the laity is a gift not only for those being ministered to, but also for those doing the ministering.

> *For those who aspire to the fullness of love, every suggestion that shows them a clearer or quicker way to that goal is extremely valuable. Almost nobody realizes it, but in my opinion, it is just as important to help devout people become even holier — and faster — as it is to help sinners be converted. It benefits the Church just as much.* [117]

- ***Your families benefit.*** They gain access to more and diverse mentors available for conversation and accompaniment. Since parents may connect better with one person than another, a larger team frees you to discern the right fit for pairing families with mentors. This gives them a better experience and an immediate connection into the larger parish following the Baptism of their child.

Perhaps, you're thinking: "Of course, that sounds fantastic, but I already have trouble keeping the scant volunteers I have. Where do I find new individuals and when do I have time?" Here are a few principles to help you find potential catechists, discern if they fit the ministry team, and retain them for the long haul. (We like building teams, but even we don't want to start from scratch every year):

1. **Remember ABCs ("Always Be Contacting").** The influence of liturgical and academic calendars — critical as they both are — can sometimes become a hindrance to effectively finding

catechists. Our planning pattern (summer prep and recruit, fall launch, winter maintenance, Christmas break, Easter to Pentecost sacrament-marathon, spring wrap up, wash, rinse, and repeat) means we primarily look for catechists in the summer, then train them for a fall program launch. This is a very short amount of time! It also severely limits candidate options. Instead, remember that recruiting potential catechists can (and should) happen year-round. You're not always looking for someone who can guide a group through robust doctrinal teaching (though *yay!* if you find some), but, rather, for a faithful disciple who can sit with someone who has welcomed a bundle of joy along with a bundle of new needs and questions. The steps are simple:

a. ***Pray.*** Ask the Holy Spirit to bring you the right workers for His vineyard.

b. ***Meet more people.*** Especially if you're introverted, make it a point to talk with parish members you haven't met. Expand your contact list. *Pay attention to people the Holy Spirit places around you.*

c. ***Ask good questions and listen intentionally.*** If you sense a particular charism or strength, share more about your ministry and gauge their interest level. Ask if they might want to learn more. *Do not ask them to join the team yet.*

d. ***Meet with them one-on-one (or with another team member). Treat them to coffee.*** Build relationships. Look for their gifts and desires, as well as reasons you may *not* want them to serve. Be honest about the commitment and challenges, as well as benefits. *Do not ask them to join the team yet.*

e. ***Invite them to "come and see" where (if anywhere) the Lord might be calling them to serve on the team.*** Let them witness the ministry in action and share with them what opportunities exist. They may be aware of the need for catechists, but may not know about prayer support, hospitality and welcoming, or other areas of need. *Do not ask them to join the team yet.*

- f. ***If comfortable, extend an offer to join the ministerial team.*** Two good conversations and an observation are usually enough to discern the right fit. You'd be surprised at how many people want to serve our Lord, but have never been personally invited to do so in a specific way. *Now you may ask them to join the team!*

- g. ***Give them time to answer.*** A thoughtful "no" is better than a rushed "yes."

    - i. ***If they accept, begin training by letting them shadow you.*** Rather than send them home with a book or slideshow, keep it simple (like Jesus did) and invite them to watch you work in the vineyard, such as your next baptismal session or interview. This lets you onboard a new team member at any time, let them witness ministry in action, and keep them from feeling alone or overwhelmed.

    - ii. ***If they decline, ask them if they know anyone else who may be a good fit.*** Don't be afraid to solicit their connections and recommendations.

- h. ***Above all, pray with and for them.*** You can never outdo the Holy Spirit's discernment and encouragement.

2. **Don't Fear Filtering.** Remember you are not just looking for any person, you are looking for the *right* person — the person God has called to *this* ministry and the team you are building with the help of the Holy Spirit. You're looking for more than a warm, baptized, breathing body (thus, the reminders not to invite them to the team until you've done some filtering)! In your conversations, you may find that this person is not the right fit for the ministry or the team. This does not mean your job is to send them packing. Trust that they are listening to the Holy Spirit and sincerely desire to join the mission of the Church. Barring any major red flags or reservations (which you may want to share with your pastor, in case the person looks to join other parish ministries), redirect

them to ministry that may be a better fit. God is never desperate, and we shouldn't be either. You are filtering the right person into the ministry, as well as filtering the wrong person out of the ministry and, God willing, into a ministry where they would flourish. Filtering has the added advantage of positioning the ministry you coordinate as something attractive and worth doing. Most of us don't want to be part of a team where *anyone* can join, regardless of qualification or commitment. Our parents and families are trusting the Church to be part of raising their child in faith. They deserve the absolute best we can offer.

FIELD NOTES—with Dino Durando

"I have found it very helpful to 'broadcast' through the parish, through various means, that catechetical work is both important and not something everyone can do well. This applies a marketing approach, making people more inclined to want to do it, especially when they are asked. They come to think: 'This person thinks I have something important and special to contribute' rather than 'I'm being asked to do one more thing that I don't have time to do.'"

What about Mass and bulletin announcements? Although large-scale invites to ministry aren't nearly as fruitful as personal invites (remember Jesus' methodology), they are a legitimate avenue for recruiting. Feel free to advertise in these places, but don't promise a role, until you've been able to meet with any potential catechist.

3. **Invest in catechists first.** As the team grows, your ministry approach needs to do the same. When you were alone, you were always working on the "ground floor," just you and your families. When you have a team (even one catechist counts as a team), investing in them becomes your new priority. Stay close with your catechists. Invest in their emotional struggles, ministerially and personally. Build them up by praying with them and teaching them deeper doctrine, as in ongoing formation. This will keep your catechists strong, prevent their burnout, and yield higher long-term retention. Ultimately, if you take care of your catechists, your catechists will take care of your parish's families (and they will do it in whatever way you did for them). For example, say you invest in five catechists, then they each invest in five families preparing for baptism. That's 25 families being ministered to, *without you having to do all the ministering.* Congratulations! You've become a personal microcosm of the Church in your own parish. You are embodying the multiplication of the loaves and fishes. With a slight change in approach, you've become part of something very special, perhaps even miraculous.

FROM THE DIRECTORY

". . . [T]he Church feels the duty of forming its catechists in the art of personal accompaniment, both by proposing to them the experience of being accompanied in order to grow in discipleship, and by enabling them and sending them to accompany their brothers." [118]

❈ Workshop This Chapter ❈

This task is simple, but productive. Grab something to write with. Then use the prompts below to make three different lists. This will help jog your memory and get you thinking about potential catechists that may not have crossed your mind yet. You don't need to do anything with these names yet. Just get them out of your brain and on the page!

- *Low Hanging Fruit.* For this list, think about people in your own circle — people who are on board with the mission of Jesus and who you get along with well, even if they don't attend your own parish. Some of them may already be serving, but some may not. These are easy asks for potential catechists.

- *On Your Tiptoes.* Think about people you are acquainted with. Perhaps, people you see at Mass or encounter every once in a while. They're not actively involved, but they're present. These may be worth an initial conversation with.

- *Grab a Ladder.* Sometimes the best fruit is at the top, but it takes a bit more effort to pick it. For this last list, write down any of the people or places you haven't necessarily considered looking for catechists. Be creative and think outside of the box! The Holy Spirit may bring a few people to mind, as well.

For additional information on this, we recommend the *Franciscan at Home* workshops "Recruiting, Training, and Forming Catechists I" and "Recruiting, Training, and Forming Catechists II."

FIELD NOTES—with Lori Smith

"When I attend any parish function, I always ask the Holy Spirit to show me who He would like to invite to serve in this ministry. 'Who Lord, would you like for me to invite to serve on our team on Your behalf? You know what we need and where we need them.' I've even done this on my way to Mass, and on more than one occasion I've received a strong interior prompting to invite someone that I would never have thought of to consider joining our team — and *every single time* it has been a total win for us, for those we serve, and for the new team member. *They even thank me for asking them, seriously!* I tell them, 'It wasn't me who invited you to serve, it was the Lord. He prompted me to invite you, because He knows your gifts and He knows they are needed on this team. Thank you for your 'yes' to Him!'"

The Need:

Skills for Building Lasting Relationships with Families

When any parent asks to have his or her child baptized, we must remember we are looking at a *person* first, then a parent. Every parent has a story, struggles, dreams, and desires. Do we truly know them? If not, why would they trust us to be the community that helps them raise their child in faith? In her book, *Forming Intentional Disciples*, Sherry Weddell describes five thresholds to help us identify benchmarks on a person's conversion journey. Just as a monarch moves from egg to caterpillar to chrysalis to butterfly, people exploring faith move through identifiable (though not always perfectly linear) phases. The first of these phases is *trust* — having a positive association with Jesus, the Church, a Christian, or something related. Many people (even baptized Catholics) approach us with little or lost trust. If we sense hesitancy, resistance, or lack of interest, then the first step is to build a bridge of trust, one human being to another. Here's how:

Skill 1: Learn to Ask Great Questions

Poor questions get poor answers. Great questions get great answers. Often the difference between them is a simple reframing. When we avoid closed questions ("Do you like Thai food?") or leading questions ("You like Mexican food, right?") and instead ask open-ended questions ("What kind of food do you like to eat?"), we will get open-ended answers. Sometimes even a story. Although closed and leading questions can't and shouldn't be avoided altogether (sometimes you just need a "yes" or "no"), open-ended questions are the ones that build bridges of trust. Here are a few examples of reframed questions:

- When were you baptized? → Would you tell me more about what your faith experience was like when you were growing up?

- Do you have any questions on what you're supposed to do during the Baptism? → How are you feeling about the big day?

- Do you know what the graces of Baptism are? → What about the sacrament is special to you? What is your hope and desire for your child in all of this?

RESOURCE RECOMMENDATION

Wish you could take a class on asking good questions? Now you can! Check out the *Catechetical Institute's* workshop on "Building the Mentoring Relationship: Asking Good Questions" for a practical online training in the art of excellent inquiry.

Skill 2: Learn to Be an Expert Listener

Once we've upped our question-asking game, it's just as critical to listen well to the answers we receive. Have you ever been in a conversation where the other party is so busy thinking about their pre-rehearsed schtick that they don't pay attention to what you're actually saying? They are "walking answers" to questions no one asked . . . and they are frustrating. If we're honest, all of us have been "that person" at some point. (When you're excited about the faith, it's hard to keep from proclaiming it!) But effective catechesis is shaped more by listening than by lecturing. This requires a subtle shift toward excitement about *their* faith, no matter how small or shallow. Then, instead of being the "sage on the stage," we can be immediately relevant to *this* family.

- Where in *this person's life* has God been speaking to him or to her?

- Do we notice how the Holy Spirit is working in this family's life? Can we point it out to them?

- Could we show them where God desires to do more for *them*?

- How does the 2,000-year history of God's family, of the Church, affect the next 20 years for *this* family?

If we listen effectively to *this* family's story, we earn the right to proclaim *God's* family story. After all, if interwoven properly, one day it will be the same.

RESOURCE RECOMMENDATION

Need help becoming a better listener? You're not alone! We'd encourage you to take the *Catechetical Institute's* workshop on "Building the Mentoring Relationship: Empathic Listening" to practice and hone your skillset in this critical area.

Skill 3: Practice the Art of Individual Accompaniment

Building relational trust with anyone is difficult, but it's nearly impossible to do in an (exclusively) group setting. In addition to cultivating opportunities for community, we need to carve out time for intimacy with parents preparing for their child's Baptism. Many of Christ's individual encounters with people happened before or after the "group meeting." Think of Nathaniel. The rich young ruler. The woman at the well. One-on-one encounters allow for conversations that provide deeper insight into the lives of each family and consequently better direction for how to best minister to their unique needs. Marriage preparation almost always includes an individual component (could you imagine if marriage preparation only happened in a group setting?), so Baptism preparation is to feature this, as well.

RESOURCE RECOMMENDATION

How do you walk with others on their journey of conversion? The *Catechetical Institute's* workshop on "Being Guided and Guiding Souls" teaches the gentle art of accompaniment, largely by first examining our own memories of being spiritually guided.

❧ Workshop This Chapter ❧

Ready to put these skills into practice? For this task, conduct a personal interview or "home visit" with a family currently preparing for Baptism in your parish. This is an excellent "best practice," but for now, do it just once. Begin by scheduling your meeting — at the parish, in their home, at a coffee shop, virtually, or by phone. If they have the baby or other children, invite them along (bring some toys or an activity), offer childcare if you're able, or schedule your chat during a time, when they already have childcare or after their kids have gone to bed. If possible, invite another team member to join you for the interview (best way to learn is "on the job").

When you meet, bring the sample list of questions below, a pen, and a notepad. Not one filled with your notes, but a blank one for you to take notes about them. (You don't need a literal notepad if that seems weird, but you get the gist). You're there to learn about them. What do you see, hear, and feel during the conversation? Listen not only to the words coming out of their mouths, but also to the things they may not be saying. If you're in their home, spend some time taking it in. Do the decorations, family photos, and books on the shelves tell you anything about what's important to them or reflect the Catholic faith? Remember this isn't a catechetical quiz. See if you can discover anything about their personal or family history.

Reframe closed or leading questions into open-ended questions that let them tell you a story. Be ready with follow-up variations (sometimes asking the same question with different language helps). You may get decent catechetical answers, but more importantly you'll get a more comprehensive look at what may be lacking for this family cognitively, emotionally, and spiritually, which means you can meet those needs more directly.

After you've completed your interview, write one to two paragraphs in the space after the list of questions recounting your experience and what you took away from it. Remember: You shouldn't ask *all* of these questions. Pick one or two to start and follow the natural flow of conversation.

Sample Interview Questions for Interview with Family

- How did you choose your child's name? Tell me the story!
- Who does your child look most like? (be sensitive to single parents)
- What does parenting look for you right now? What's been easy? What's been difficult?
- How has your child been sleeping?
- What's the newest skill or milestone they've reached? (crawling, first tooth, and so on)?
- Do you have any special family traditions you've begun or implemented?
- What are important celebrations or holidays for your family?
- What types of things are important to you, as you raise your family?
- What were your parents like when you were a child?
- Have you been living in [insert city] for long? If not,
    - Where are you from?
    - What brought you here?

- How often do you get back home?
- Do you keep in touch with family?

* If they volunteer any connection to having had a sacrament at the parish, ask: Were your godparents or grandparents able to be there? Were they Catholic? What parish did they worship at?

* Were you ever involved in activities connected to the parish (youth groups, scouts, and so on)?

* What was your faith experience growing up? Present or absent? Positive or negative?

* What has been your experience with this own parish? Good, bad, or otherwise.

* What brings you to this parish for Baptism? Why do you desire to baptize your child?

* What about this sacrament is special to you?

* What is the highest and best thing you desire for this child?

* What is the highest and best thing you desire for your family?

* What is the highest and best thing you desire for *you*?

* If you could put it into words, how would you describe your relationship with Christ to this point in your life?[119]

* What questions do you have for me?

FIELD NOTES—with Margaret Wickware

"I constantly try to build connection with families. Conversations may be totally unrelated to the sacrament itself. Recently, one young father did not want to be involved in our virtual sessions. But during the third session, his wife wasn't feeling well, and he talked the entire time! Another man—all of his friends are of different faiths or agnostic, so he can't talk about his faith, he doesn't have the language. I have a Russian Orthodox woman whose husband is Catholic. I sent her a little message saying 'Happy Easter' on the day the Orthodox celebrate Easter. For families interested in faith and science, I send them to the Thomistic Institute. If they've traveled a lot and talked about Spain, I connect them to Bishop Robert Barron and his 'Pivotal Players' series on Ignatius of Loyola. It's not like I don't talk about God when I'm developing these relationships. But this is seed-planting for the future of our parish, not a course or program. Even in perfect soil, seeds need water and sunlight to flourish. We all want our children to flourish — we want the best for our child — so we ask ourselves: how can we help this child to flourish? It's not a class, it's a relationship."

The Co-Laborers:
Working with Godparents

If you've ever prepared a family for Baptism, you are probably familiar with the godparents' qualifications, which your family's selections may or may not meet. Navigating these dynamics can be tricky, but are also ripe with opportunity for growth, conversion, and relationship. How do we stay compassionate, while holding to the Church's expectations? How do we guide parents toward a selection of godparents who will actively support them in this new life? How do we meaningfully involve godparents in the process both before and after Baptism day? We have a few suggestions:

First, let's look at what is truly *required* to be a godparent, taken from the *Code of Canon Law*:

(Canon 872) In so far as possible, a person to be baptized is to be given a sponsor who assists an adult in Christian initiation or together with the parents presents an infant for Baptism. A sponsor also helps the baptized person to lead a Christian life in keeping with Baptism and to fulfill faithfully the obligations inherent in it.

Working with Godparents

(Canon 873) There is to be only one male sponsor or one female sponsor or one of each.

(Canon 874.1) To be permitted to take on the function of a sponsor a person must:

1. Be designated by the one to be baptized, by the parents or the person who takes their place, or in their absence by the pastor or minister and have the aptitude and intention of fulfilling this function;

2. Have completed the sixteenth year of age, unless the diocesan bishop has established another age, or the pastor or minister has granted an exception for a just cause;

3. Be a Catholic who has been confirmed and has already received the Most Holy Sacrament of the Eucharist and who leads a life of faith in keeping with the function to be taken on;[120]

4. Not be bound by any canonical penalty legitimately imposed or declared;[121] and

5. Not be the father or mother of the one to be baptized.

(Canon 874.2) A baptized person who belongs to a non-Catholic ecclesial community is not to participate except together with a Catholic sponsor and then only as a witness of the Baptism.

Although these requirements are basic, they can still *feel* burdensome for parents. The *Directory for Catechesis* recognizes that "... often the choice of godparents is not motivated by faith but based on family or social customs ...." [122] putting parents in the tough spot of finding godparents who meet family expectations *and* check the "church boxes." We must be sensitive to this decision-making process (choosing godparents can come with heaps of familial guilt), knowing that new parents are often navigating new boundaries, as they make important decisions about how *they* want to parent, all the while receiving the lion's share of unsolicited advice. We should also remember that godparents don't usually apply for the job — they're asked. Although occasionally someone will insist upon taking the role (and most of us aren't worried about their qualifications), when parents select godparents, it's because they observed at least *something* they considered to be good, wholesome, and Christian (whether their assessment is accurate is beside the point for the time being).

FROM THE DIRECTORY

"In the journey of initiation into the Christian life, the Church calls for a reevaluation of the identity and mission of the godfather and godmother, as support for the educational effort of the parents. Their task is 'to show the candidates how to practice the Gospel in personal and social life, to sustain the candidates in moments of hesitancy and anxiety, to bear witness, and to guide the candidates' progress in the baptismal life.'" [123]

What might this look like in practice? Here are a few tips or "best practices" to assist parents in their selection process:

- *Ensure that parents know the qualifications for godparents upfront.* Consider sharing the qualifications (in simple language) wherever you provide general information about Baptism. This also gives the parents an easy way to direct potential godparents to the qualifications. The *Directory* affirms that these requirements "should have been made clear in the discussion that precedes selection." [124] They needn't be a deterrent, but they should never be a surprise.

- *Use tentative language when asking parents to submit godparent selections.* Although this isn't a job application, employ a similar approach. Words like "request," "apply," "suggest," "candidates," "potential," and so on, all convey the message that criteria must be met before godparent selection can be approved.

- *Preemptively address misunderstandings.* For example, in some cultures, godparents are the ones who take legal custody of the children if both parents were to die. Although godparents *can* be designated as legal guardians, parents should be relieved to know these are two separate roles, not interchangeable.

- *Consider interviewing potential godparents.* A brief chat, in person or on the phone, will let you vet godparents in just a few minutes. It also gives you the chance to hear their story and build relationship. (Some priests or catechetical leaders require a potential godparent's parish to submit a form verifying they are actively practicing the faith; although we understand the reasoning, the state of parishes today — fewer priests, more lay leaders, clusters, and so on — can also make this cumbersome on both ends).

- *Offer alternatives.* When objective requirements are absent or potential godparents refuse to accept the responsibility, the *Directory* urges us to handle the situation "with great pastoral care." If the family agrees, "godparents can be chosen from among the pastoral workers (catechists, teachers, organizers) who stand as witnesses of faith and of ecclesial presence." [125] Have a few people from your parish in mind that you can offer as options!

- *View the godparents as part of the family you are ministering to.* Avoid seeing godparents as simply a means to an end. Although there are requirements to fulfill, "[t]hose who are selected for this role often feel called upon to reawaken their baptismal faith and to initiate a renewed journey of commitment and witness." [126] Keep this in mind, asking the Holy Spirit to show you how to nurture *their* seed of faith, however small or neglected.

❈ Workshop This Chapter ❈

In light of the godparents' responsibility, the *Directory* challenges us to "indicate, with discernment and a creative spirit, pathways of catechesis, for godparents, which may help them to rediscover the gift of faith and of belonging to the Church." [127] For this task, call upon your creative spirit (and the Holy Spirit) to conceive:

- Three potential ideas for how you could more meaningfully involve godparents in the baptismal preparation process you *already* offer.

- One potential idea for how you could meaningfully involve godparents in a *new* way, either before or after Baptism.

- One potential idea for how you could minister directly *to* the godparents in their unique role.

Note your ideas above, then bring them to your team. Are there any you could easily implement in the next few months? Decide together which idea makes the most sense, spend time praying about it, and eventually agree upon a timeline for implementation. Perhaps, a team member or two could even be in charge of serving and forming godparents as an extension of your infant baptismal preparation. There is great potential in this area to bring lost sheep back into the fold!

The Parents:
Meeting the Unique Needs of Mothers and Fathers

BEING A NEW PARENT IN TODAY'S WORLD IS HARD. It's why people delay it, deny it, or destroy it. It's also why when men and women *do* embrace it, we must be committed to helping them on their journey — not only the spiritual journey of sacramental preparation, but also the very real adventure of raising children in faith. In welcoming new life, their lives have changed in every way possible. The man moving from husband to head of his domestic church. The woman embodying the role of our Blessed Mother and the Church itself in her own way. The question is not whether or not they will take on these roles (by virtue of their parenthood they already have), rather — are they *aware* of taking on these roles and will they take them on well or poorly? Our assistance (or lack of) matters a great deal!

All ministry, including sacramental preparation, involves holistic and organic catechesis, meaning teaching to and accompanying the whole person with the knowledge that their many parts make a living whole. In our encounters and catechetical preparation for the sacrament, we take into account the demands of being a parent, such as sleep deprivation that affects one's mental abilities and emotional state, the physical and financial changes, and so on. Also, culturally being aware of the single-parent or two-income households becoming more prevalent means considering your schedule to meet theirs, such as duplicate sessions at different days and times. Accompanying parents means engaging in their lives and helping them to live day-to-day in the Catholic faith.

Mothers have new needs. Her body has surrendered to God's gift of new life.

Emotionally, she's given up a great deal of her social life to caring for an infant, especially if she was the first to enter motherhood. *Professionally*, she may face subtle or overt repercussions for having a child. *Mentally*, she and her husband are making hard choices about raising children on a minute-to-minute basis. Her internal monologue never shuts off. And the loudest one . . . *I'm alone.* Mothers need our help.

Fathers have new needs. New schedule. *Do I have time for the gym? For my baseball team? Probably not.* New finances. New role. *What do I know about being a dad?* New feelings. *She's with the baby, again. When was the last time we talked?* But dads often feel like they can't say anything. After all, he didn't have it as rough. There's no postpartum protocol for guys. He feels the need to be a silent pillar of strength for his family. With his network gone, he feels trapped in deafening silence with only one ruminating phrase in his ear. *I'm alone.* Fathers need our help.

As a team, knowing what you can help with and what you shouldn't help with is important. If not already done, discuss this with your team and form through your pastor and diocese a list of resources, such as counseling and healthcare, that you imagine may be needed. No matter their unique struggles, this man and woman have real, practical needs. There is a need for us to practice real, corporal works of mercy. If we want to bring them into the flock — especially if they're far off — we must begin with Christ's mercy and *incarnate* it for these precious souls. Parents coming to us for Baptism don't check their bags at the door! So instead of shoving them into a closet, what if we made room? Maybe even help them unpack? Sure, it'll take a lot more work.

Yes, it'll be much messier. But did we really expect to bear much fruit in the Lord's vineyard without offering this kind of help?

FROM THE DIRECTORY

"It is important that every Christian community take a realistic view of the heterogeneous family realities, with their ups and downs, for the sake of *accompanying them* in an adequate way and *discerning* the complexity of the situations, without giving in to forms of idealism and pessimism." [128]

". . . in the dynamic of missionary conversion catechesis with families is characterized by a style of humble understanding and by a proclamation that is concrete, not theoretical and detached from personal problems." [129]

❊ Workshop This Chapter ❊

Below you'll find lists of the corporal and spiritual works of mercy, taken from the teachings of Jesus. Since we know that Jesus frequently met physical needs often as a precursor to meeting spiritual needs, let's see if we can do the same for new mothers and fathers in our own parishes.

For the first part of this task, call upon the Holy Spirit to help you imagine one to two practical ways your parish might meet each of these *corporal* works of mercy for a new mother or new father seeking Baptism, or who has recently had their child baptized. Think outside the box, metaphorically or symbolically, as well as literally. (Note that parents already perform many of these for their own children!)

Corporal Work of Mercy	How could you meet this need for a new father?	How could you meet this need for a new mother?
Feed the Hungry		
Give Drink to the Thirsty		
Shelter the Homeless		

Visit the Sick		
Visit the Imprisoned		
Bury the Dead		
Give Alms to the Poor		

For the second part of this task, see if you can connect the dots from the parish helping meet physical needs to the parish helping meet spiritual needs. For each of the corporal works of mercy above, how could meeting *that* need potentially build a bridge to serving spiritual needs (particularly for grace available in the sacraments)?

As you think about how helping meet the physical needs can tie into forms of spiritual and pastoral care, you might find it helpful to bear in mind the traditional list of the spiritual works of mercy.

- Counseling the doubtful,
- Instructing the ignorant,
- Admonishing the sinner,
- Comforting the sorrowful,
- Forgiving injuries,
- Bearing wrongs patiently, and
- Praying for the living and the dead.

Corporal Work of Mercy	Building Spiritual Care On To This
Feed the Hungry	
Give Drink to the Thirsty	
Shelter the Homeless	
Visit the Sick	
Visit the Imprisoned	
Bury the Dead	
Give Alms to the Poor	

RESOURCE RECOMMENDATION

Pope Francis's Apostolic Exhortation "On Love in the Family," *Amoris laetitia* (translated "the joy of love") expands our awareness of the unique challenges facing modern parents. We recommend a read through of "The Experiences and Challenges of Families" (31–57) and "Love Made Fruitful" (165–198) sections.

The Holy Family:

Helping Families of Young Children Enter Into Deeper Prayer

If you don't have young children (or if that season of raising them is all but a distant memory), it's easy to forget about the constant clamor and endless neediness that surrounds parents of little ones. In particular, prayer can feel like something parents are failing at, despite their best efforts. (As sleepy newborns turn into curious toddlers and chatty preschoolers, it's hard enough to have an adult conversation, much less find an hour of prayerful silence). In this season of life, your sincere encouragement and practical guidance can go a long way for parents, who want to hear from God, but can't seem to make out His voice amidst the noise. Here are a few simple suggestions to offer your families:

At Mass. Encouraging families with young children to attend weekly Mass may seem like an easy ask, but for them, the Sunday obligation may feel more like a hardcore workout than a profound hour of worship. They probably won't hear much of the homily. They may have to wrestle their squawking toddler out before the first reading. Their kid may or may not yell out a perfectly-timed phrase during a moment of blessed silence. They may feel like a horrible parent because of it, but the reality is that it's all completely normal. Here's how you can help make the experience a little bit easier:

- **Welcome them.** Smile at them, tell them it's good they are at Mass, engage with their children, train catechists and mentors to sit near these families, ask how you can help (pastors, you can *verbally* affirm this from the sanctuary — after all, you usually have the advantage of a microphone!)

- **Offer a calm-down space.** Include a few quiet toys or books. A livestream video or audio of the Mass can be helpful, but it isn't necessary. Do note that this room is *not* to keep families out of Mass for the convenience of parishioners, but rather to give families a place to breathe and reset, before they rejoin the congregation.

- **Encourage flexibility.** Remind parents to pick a Mass time that works around meals and naptimes (even if it's at a neighboring parish), remind them they can offer each Mass as a sacrifice for a personal intention, and remind them that even if the only thing they "get" out of Mass is Jesus in the Eucharist, that really is enough - and they might even find time to pray with the Mass readings either before or after Mass.

In Life. It's much easier to care for children when you yourself feel cared for. Here a few prayerful suggestions for parents with young children:

- **Offer to watch their children.** Consider hosting a regular opportunity for parent confession, Adoration, Bible study, or catechesis that includes a child-care team.

- **Remind them their children are not an obstacle, but a pathway to prayer.** If we imitate Mary, distractions and interruptions can *become* our prayer life. Encourage parents to imagine their child as infant/toddler/preschooler Jesus, as they follow their child around. It may give them new perspective!

- **Provide solidarity.** Introduce parents to each other and let them share season-of-life fellowship. It is much easier when you know it's normal and you're not alone!

- **Teach basic family prayers.** Don't take for granted that families know the *Hail Mary* or to say a prayer before meals or bedtime. Teach them little, doable ways to incorporate faith into their domestic church.

- **Introduce them to parent saints.** Obviously, the Holy Family — Mary and Joseph — but there are others, as well! Offer multiple examples of sanctity and how it happens in the monotony of everyday life. (Consider taking the *Catechetical Institute* workshop on "Parent Saints.")

- **Teach them how to read the Bible.** Begin in small ways (for example, the table of contents) or where to begin (perhaps, the Gospels or an epistle). Show them how the Living Word still speaks to them today.

- ***Personally*** **invite them to events.** Let them know they are welcome in the parish community. Even when they say no, they will remember being asked.

- **Ask how you can pray for them.** Then do it, not later, but right then and there, in person or on the phone. Model the simple language of talking to the Father.

Then little children were being brought to him in order that he might lay his hands on them and pray. The disciples spoke sternly to those who brought them; but Jesus said, "Let the little children come to me, and do not stop them; for it is to such as these that the kingdom of heaven belongs." [130]

❊ Workshop This Chapter ❊

The following excerpt is taken from a series titled "RCIA: Questions, Answers, Issues and Advice" in *The Sower,* which is now the *Catechetical Review,* the Franciscan University of Steubenville's catechetical publication. The question that Dr. William Keimig answers is "Beyond Mystagogy: Why is the Neophyte Year of a New Catholic so Important?" Although this article was intended for those in catechumenal (OCIA) ministry, there are significant takeaways for us in infant baptismal preparation. As you read, anytime you see the word "neophyte," replace it in your own mind with "parent."

> Most Catholics absent on Sunday morning, even 'cradle Catholics,' don't 'fall away,' they drift away. Little by little a *lack of spiritual support and accountability* begets laxity in the life of faith, until only the name Catholic remains . . .
>
> Care should be taken especially in the neophyte year to help them to grow and mature in the Christian life and to develop a genuine Catholic worldview . . .
>
> As their minds and hearts continue to be fed on Scripture and the truths of the faith, and are transformed by the graces received in the sacraments, the fullness of Catholic truth gradually permeates all areas of their thinking. They may find themselves more sensitive to issues concerning life, human dignity, social justice, the value of suffering, the importance of family and vocation, the dignity of labor, and stewardship of the natural world. The list can go on to touch every aspect of human life and society.
>
> This process takes time. **It usually takes three to five years** for neophytes to consistently think and feel like Catholics. Issues may come up, not necessarily entirely new

but presenting themselves in a new light, or issues may arise that they had never dealt with before, and suddenly they surprise themselves by looking at them in a new way because of their Catholic formation.

Care should be taken to be sure that each neophyte is securely established in the life of the parish during their first year as Catholics. The difficulties of this year can be very great. These fledgling Catholics cannot be neglected or forgotten . . .

It would be easy to adopt an attitude that says, 'These are adults. If they don't come, it's not my responsibility.' While it is true that each person is ultimately responsible for his or her own spiritual progress, recall that the author of the Book of Hebrews recognized the newly-initiated as needing spiritual milk, not yet ready for food (see Hebrews 5:12–14). Saint Paul saw himself as a spiritual father to the Christian communities he founded (see 1 Corinthian 4:15; 1 Thessalonians 2:11).[131]

After you've read through this excerpt, spend some time reflecting on your *own* spiritual journey as a Catholic. Think about any moments or circumstances that have surprised you, moments where you saw your own worldview change, moments when you were more sensitive to something than you had been in the past, and so on. How is your practice as a Catholic *now* different from how it was several years ago? Write some brief notes reflecting on these questions. Then, say a prayer for all of the families currently in your parish who are in this "neophyte" phase. Ask the Holy Spirit to bless them, open their hearts to deeper conversion, and help your parish become a place where they can become deeply rooted in faith and in community.

The Window of Opportunity:

Ministering to Families with Children Under Six

... [F]amilies are not a problem, they are first and foremost an opportunity. [132]

EVEN WITH ALL ITS JOYS, THE FIRST FIVE *YEARS* OF PARENTING can be a *grind*. Some politely label it "the active stage" of parenting. For others it's "the tunnel." Whatever you call it, it's not for the fainthearted! As we think about creating formational opportunities for this season, we can't forget that parenting children 0–5 is particularly demanding and (in modern culture) profoundly isolating. Our efforts should always keep this in mind. They may have come to us only for a sacrament, not realizing that we have that *and* more! They may initially come to meet a spiritual or social obligation, not knowing how much the faith of the Church can help them with life and parenting. Remembering back to Step Four's "Field Notes" from

Dr. Joseph White — the *primary* goal for this season is to help families find community, the kind that provides support, socialization, and solidarity, so that they can say: "Thank goodness, I'm not alone in my woes!" If they don't find it at the parish, they *will* find it somewhere else (soccer, dance, playgroup, and so on). We can consider some opportunities for parents only (with childcare offered) and some opportunities for children only, but in general, we should lean heavily toward offering opportunities that the whole family can easily attend *together*.

FROM THE DIRECTORY

"*Early childhood*, or pre-school age, is a definitive time for the discovery of religious reality, during which children learn from their parents and from the environment of life an attitude of openness and acceptance or of aversion and exclusion toward God . . . When from an early age the child is in contact, in the family or in other surroundings in which it grows, with different aspects of the Christian life, he learns and internalizes an initial form of *religious socialization* in preparation for the forms that come later . . ." [133]

RESOURCE RECOMMENDATION

Interested in learning more about this stage of development? Drawing from Dr. Maria Montessori's "sensitive periods", the *Catechetical Institute* workshop "Faith & Moral Development: Ages 3–6" presented by Dr. Gerard O'Shea helps us build on what naturally occurs in the mind and heart of young children, so they can be caught up into the Heart of Jesus. "And he took them in his arms and blessed them . . ." [134]

FIELD NOTES—with Carol Ann Harnett

"In this modern era there's so many choices (sports, dance, and so on) compared to when I was growing up. What parents need is to have a connection to the Church. The universal Church yes, bu,t they need to connect to the universal Church *through* the local parish. They need to feel that this is *their* parish, that they belong. As I think back to the parish where I brought my children up, we had mother's luncheons, mothers and toddlers group — it wasn't a deliberate ministry to families, there was just a lot going on. I like to invite them to events that interest them. They might not always be 'religious events,' but they have faith at its core, because God created us as community and as family. There needs to be some way where people who come through the door to have their children baptized can also come through the door for other reasons." [135]

❦ Workshop This Chapter ❦

For this task, we're going to help you mine the expert advice lingering under the surface in your own parish. Start by enlisting your team to help you make a list of parish families who are currently[136] raising children 0–5 years old. Next, reach out to at least one of them (though more is better) and ask if they'd be willing to give you and your team some ideas about how to better support families with young children, particularly in faith and prayer. (This is an excellent place to invite a team member into planning and feedback.) Make this easy on the family — give them the option to voice their thoughts via email or phone, or bring their family a meal or treat them to ice cream while you chat (you will be interrupted many times, but it will be okay). And as always, invite a team member to come with you! Never go alone; go two-by-two.

Using the "asking good questions" skills from page 160, listen for their struggles, as well as opportunities to support them in those struggles. Take notes in the space below. If their children are closer to five, ask what *would* have been helpful to them in those earlier years of parenting. Last, thank them for their time and for their vocation to raising children in faith!

After your conversation, step back and look at everything your parish currently has to offer: every group, every liturgy, every ministry. Of parish offerings, formal or casual, which ones could minister to families with young children in the time between Baptism and the beginning of more formal faith formation programs?

After interviewing this family, what ideas do you and your team have for *additional* offerings to meet these needs? Take some time to come up with two to three *new* ideas you or your team members would like to bring to your pastor, your baptismal prep team, or your parish council for consideration. Remember, they don't need to be big, fancy, expensive, or formal. Casually connecting a new family with a more experienced family from the parish can accomplish the same objective as offering a weekly facilitated parent-child group.

And remember, you don't need to be in charge of launching these! You are simply mining for ideas. We've found that "we invest in what we create" is a very true maxim. Think of this interview process as an opportunity to awaken the creative spirit within your parish community. If you notice that someone has passion for a particular idea or outreach, rather than adding it to your already too-long to-do list, encourage them to pursue the idea and be the wind beneath their wings!

Use the space provided to write down any ideas you or your team come up with.

The Village:

Involving Your Parish Community in Baptism Preparation

YOU'VE HEARD THE AFRICAN PROVERB EXPRESSION, "IT takes a village to raise a child," but this becomes especially true when the "child" in question is the whole family. *You* may have been formally tasked with baptismal preparation, but it is *not* your responsibility to singlehandedly minister to all families going through baptismal preparation and beyond. Even if you wanted to do it yourself, you can't and shouldn't, because it's too big and it's not meant for just one person. Notably, it would deprive the community of its evangelical responsibility and accompanying joys. Whether your parish community is big or small, active or inactive, Baptism must, by its very nature, incorporate and initiate families into that particular community.

> *One of the most valid criteria in the process of adult catechesis, but which is often overlooked, is the involvement of the community which welcomes and sustains adults. Adults do not grow in faith primarily by learning concepts, but by sharing the life of the Christian community, of which adults are members who both give and receive from the community.* [137]

Involving Your Parish Community in Baptism Preparation

Here are some of the key players within your own parish "village":

- **Your Pastor.** We cannot stress how critical it is to be unified with the bishop and those he has assigned to be your priest(s) and pastor. As shepherds, they are responsible for the souls and spiritual growth of their people (not only within the church building, but also the entire geographical parish), as well as administration of the sacraments. By virtue of his God-given authority, what your priest initiates and pursues is what will bear the most fruit. For example, if the pastor *expects* adults within the community to give of themselves in some way (and verbalizes this consistently), the community will eventually follow. If you have not already done so, speak with your pastor (perhaps treat him to coffee, lunch, or dinner) to discover his vision for baptismal preparation and ongoing formation, then work to unite your vision with his. (If you *are* the pastor, it is hoped that you are already united on this point!)

- **Parish Catechists.** Even if they're not explicitly involved in baptismal preparation, build relationships and collaborate with fellow catechists or ministers in your parish. Let them know what's happening with parents you encounter and ask for their opinion on how to cultivate follow through. A current men or women's group, Bible study, or possibly OCIA may be the perfect next step for a family.

- **Parish Families.** There are many members of your parish congregation who would make excellent friends or mentors to families in baptismal preparation (especially parents with kids a bit older). They may not be able to commit to teaching weekly classes, but they could invite a new family to their house for dinner. Get to know these parishioners, let them know they've stood out to you, and personally invite them to consider walking alongside others (no public speaking required) — perhaps by offering childcare, setting up community events, or meeting individually with families. Yes, families are busy, but asking them to give of themselves is not simply another obligation, but rather an opportunity for their spiritual growth.

- **Parish "Grandparents."** Although there is great value in families connecting with others in the same season-of-life, there is also great value in intergenerational relationships. Consider recruiting empty nesters to act as spiritual moms, dads, or mentors. Or ask homebound members of your parish or that faithful group of Little Old Church Ladies to do what they do best: pray for these families, by name. Many would be honored to help, especially in a season of life where they may not feel as valuable or able to contribute as they once did.

When involving your parish village in baptismal preparation, seek not only their labor (for example, "here, can you do this job?"), but also their Spirit-inspired ideas and contributions. In general, never forget the power of a *personal invitation* as opposed to a generic posting or announcement. Additionally, look for people or places *already* bearing fruit and seek to integrate families there first. If you do need to start something new, remember that it does not need to be large, formal, structured, or expensive and *you* do not necessarily need to be the person who starts it. Call upon the charisms of your community, inviting them to assess the problem *with* you (don't assume they see the needs of families yet). If any of us saw a child physically struggling to tie their shoes, or Heaven forbid, with basic needs or safety, we wouldn't hesitate to help. And what is an unevangelized or disconnected family if not a spiritually struggling child in God's family? Even if it has been difficult for you to recruit or retain volunteers, don't hesitate to keep asking.

FROM THE DIRECTORY

"Since the Christian community is a structural element of the catechetical process for the adult and not only its setting, it is necessary that it be capable of renewal, allowing itself to be challenged by the adults of today and their particular concerns, as well as being a place of welcome, presence, and support." [138]

❦ Workshop This Chapter ❦

This chapter may be about involving the village in baptismal prep, but this task has a bit of twist. Given the state of the modern parish, we cannot take it for granted that *you* feel a sense of welcome, presence, and support in your parish. Sure, you're in ministry. You're leading the pack. You're offering blood, sweat, and tears in the spiritual struggle for the salvation of souls. But do you feel like you *belong*? Do you have a community around *you*? Are there people you can call or text for help when *you're* the one who feels alone, drowning in your own set of urgent needs? The community is not something you create only for others. It is something that you are a part of. And before you can authentically invite others into that community, you need to have experienced it for yourself.

For this task, go and sit with Jesus in the Blessed Sacrament for twenty or thirty minutes. Talk to Him about your parish community and how you feel within it. If you feel at home, thank Him. If you feel frustrated, vent. If you feel left out, cry. Or whatever expression feels necessary. As a son or daughter of God, before you ever minister to another soul, first offer up your own sincere needs and desires, asking the Father to sweep you up into the loving community of the Trinity — not only in the life to come, but also in this life, too.

The Exceptions to the Rule:

Ministering in Special Situations

Special Family Situations

- Baptism Preparation with Single Parents
- Baptism Preparation with Unmarried Parents
- Baptism Preparation with Grandparents
- Baptism Preparation with Parents of Subsequent Children (second, third, fourth, and so on)

Special Baptismal Situations

- Baptism for Older Children (but not yet at the age of reason)
- Baptism for Older Children (at or above the age of reason)
- Baptism for Older Children with Developmental Disabilities
- Cases of Miscarriage, Stillbirth, or Infant Loss

Special Parish Situations

- Extremely Small Parishes (under 100 families)
- Extremely Large Parishes (over 1,000 families)
- Limited Budgets
- Urban Parishes
- Rural Parishes
- Ethnically Diverse Parishes

FROM THE DIRECTORY

"There is a tremendous increase in conjugal and family crises . . . With concern, respect, and pastoral solicitude, the Church wants to accompany those children who are marked by a wounded love, who find themselves in the most fragile condition, restoring their trust and hope . . . It is important that every Christian community take a realistic view of the heterogenous family realities, with their ups and downs, for the sake of *accompanying them* in an adequate way and *discerning* the complexity of the situations, without giving in to forms of idealism and pessimism . . . In addition to personal spiritual accompaniment, catechists should find ways and means to foster the participation of these brothers in catechesis as well, in specific groups made up of persons who share the same conjugal or family experience or in other pre-existing groups of families or adults." [139]

Q. How do I navigate single-parent situations with sensitivity?

A. This question already presents a generalization, since there are many reasons — most not by choice — why a person might be single parenting (separation, divorce, abuse, mental health, physical health, death, war, and so on). Regardless of cause, single parents must tackle this massive task without the support and relief of their spouse, leaving them more prone to burnout and discouragement, often working more than one literal job to make ends meet. That said, although they may be *single* parenting, they are not alone, and God's Presence and grace is always available to them in parenting. Be attentive to extra practical needs. Additionally, be sensitive to any complicated marital situations (separation or divorce) and be prepared to work with both parents individually or together, at whatever level they are comfortable, knowing your limitations and relying on referrals from your parish's list of resources for things like counseling.

The most critical thing to remember here is attunement to the needs of the individual parent in front of you. Ask open-ended questions, solicit their story, and get a sense of their needs due to their unique situation. Don't assume you know what they need before they tell you. They may have help in some areas, but not in others. No matter what:

- Applaud them for their effort and offer extra accommodation when you can.

- Make childcare a priority.

- Avoid any need for an in-person meeting that could be an email, phone call, or text. With younger parents, you may find that they don't read their emails and their voicemail box is full, meaning a text is best. If you have access to a parish texting service, you can use that, or you can give out your cell number. This may mean they contact you "after parish hours." You don't have to respond until later, but the effort to contact them on their timeframe (it's so much easier to communicate after kids have gone to bed!) pays off exponentially.

- Allow for a substitute (relative, friend from Church) to stand-in at meetings, if necessary.

- Check in personally to see if they have specific material or spiritual needs.

- Minister to them the same way you would to any parents: connect them with someone in the parish in similar circumstances. The devil loves to heap extra shame and isolation on single parents. Don't let him get a foothold. Show parents they are not alone and you take seriously God's plan for their life, even if it is unfolding differently than anticipated.

Better yet, provided they are living out the Church's teaching faithfully, consider inviting those same parish members (single parents) to be active participants on your team! You will find that irregular situations are becoming the rule, not the exception, and you can begin to prepare your parish even now. Invoke and expect to encounter the Holy Spirit's creativity in meeting needs.

Saint Margaret of Cortona, patron of single mothers, pray for our single parents and their children.

Saint Eugene de Mazenod, patron of divorced people, pray for our divorced parents and for their children.

Q. How should I work with parents asking for Baptism who are not married?

A. Believe it or not, there's nothing canonical that requires parents to be married before baptizing their baby! Many of them have never seen any marriage last, much less a faithful, sacramental one. Don't assume that an unmarried couple isn't intentional about their family life, parenting style, and religion. It's possible they've talked about these things at length, so these can be great conversation starters. Though you can't begin with the supernatural graces that flow from the Sacrament of Marriage for the education of their children (since they haven't got them), you *can* talk about those graces and plant the seed for more conversations and potential for marriage or convalidation down the road. The best thing to do here is to give these couples encounters with vibrant, faith-filled couples (in their age group, if possible) who are sacramentally married and living out those graces in raising their family. Let them witness the struggles along with the goodness, truth, and beauty firsthand.

P.S. Although the *parents* don't need to be married, it IS a requirement that the *godparents* (if married) are married sacramentally, according to the guidance of the Church. This is a great opportunity to draw on the godparents and their witness in this family's life.

Q. How do I handle a situation where grandparents present a child for Baptism?

A. With an economy often making it very challenging to avoid both parents working outside the home, it's not uncommon for grandparents to be more involved in caretaking for their grandchildren. Sometimes, this means they are the ones who request Baptism, often because the parents (their children) are not practicing the faith. In these cases, it's critical to seek the parents' authentic consent, or at least, absence of objection. If parents are willing to be involved in the preparation process, encourage, invite, and welcome them! If not, but they still consent to Baptism, there's no reason why you can't go through a similar preparation process with the grandparents. If you know other grandparents raising their grandchildren in faith within your parish community, make an intentional effort to connect them together in their unique struggles and prayers.

FROM THE DIRECTORY

"... [I]t is the *grandparents*, above all in certain cultures, who carry out a special role in the transmission of the faith to the very young. Scripture, as well, presents the faith of grandparents as a witness for their grandchildren (cf. 2 Timothy 1:5). 'The Church has always paid special attention to grandparents, recognizing them as a great treasure from both human and social, as well as religious and spiritual viewpoints.' In the face of family crisis, grandparents, who are often more deeply rooted in the Christian faith and have a past rich with experience, become important points of reference. Often, in fact, many people owe their initiation into the Christian life precisely to their grandparents. The contribution of grandparents turns out to be important in catechesis on account of both the greater amount of time they are able to dedicate and their capacity to encourage younger generations with their characteristic affection. The prayers of petition and song of praise from grandparents sustains the community in the work and struggles of life." [140]

Saints Joachim and Anne, grandparents of Jesus, pray for us!

Q. What about parents baptizing a second/third/subsequent child? What if it's been several years since their last baby? Should they go through the Baptism class again?

If you're still calling your baptismal preparation a class, then we have other things to worry about and you should go back to Step Four of this book! We get it. It's so easy for us to fall into the liability of requirements, checked boxes, and course completion certificates. It's the only way we've ever known how to evaluate if our program is successful. Unfortunately, although we're good at gauging how many people go through our programs, what we're not so great at is making them want to stay anywhere in the vicinity of our parish, once the program is over. If we want different outcomes (falling in love with Jesus, becoming His disciples, experiencing deeper conversion, engagement with the parish), then we need a different way to get there.

Let's think about this in the context of parents baptizing a baby that's not their first. Even though they've had a baby before, any time a family adds a new member to the family it creates massive upheaval, not just for the parents, but for the entire unit. Everyone is affected. Sleep schedules change, again. Finances change, again. We play a giant game of musical chairs to figure out where everyone is going to sleep, once they're sleeping with any regularity. Times of upheaval can be times of great openness and times of new urgent needs. As you work with this family, maintain the practice of an individual interview or house visit (with you, or a catechist). Spend time with them, not to give them more information, but to truly listen to them, their story, their needs, their fears, their hopes, and so on, and what they desire for baptismal preparation with *this* child. The Holy Spirit is always at work in their hearts, usually at the point of desire or openness.

And, of course, never assume the *kerygma* has been proclaimed, received, or responded to. Learn new ways to hear and share the Good News of Jesus. Even if they have dropped their nets to follow Christ, they (like us) are always in need of deeper evangelization and greater conversion. There are still patches of dry soil in our own hearts that need the seed, the rain, the sun, and the shade. Long story short, your goal is not simply that they cognitively know what's happening at Baptism. Your goal is to invite them more deeply into the community of the Trinity and of the parish. There are ten-thousand-

and-one different ways to do that. Allow the Holy Spirit to cater the approach most needed to the family in front of you. Perhaps, a catechetical refresher on Baptism *is* what they want and need most. But more likely this is a chance to grab their hand once again (if we let it go after the first baby) and start walking.

Q. Do you have tips for working with older children (not at the age of reason, but old enough to know what's going on)?

A. Despite the urging of the Rite for parents to baptize their children within the first few days or weeks after birth, it's growing increasingly common for parents to wait until the child is much older. The reasons vary. In these situations (like with any sacramental situation that is "out of the norm") remember there's usually more going on underneath the surface in the life of this family. This calls for extra care and sensitivity, both toward the parents and the child. Make an effort to build trust and learn the family's story, particularly the parents' upbringing, as it relates to faith, as well as any fears, hesitations, or resistance they may have toward the Church.

Additionally, involve the child in the preparation process as much as possible. Although they are not making the decision to be baptized, we do want them to know what's happening and why. Use age-appropriate ways of explaining the Rite, how God is welcoming them into his family, and so on. Ask questions, let them ask you questions, show books or videos, introduce them to the pastor, give a personal tour of the Church, font, vessels, and vestments. Host a rehearsal to practice where they will walk or stand, how they will get in or hold their head over the font, as well as who will be there to help them (mom, dad, godparents, and so on). It may be helpful for you or a team member to be personally present on Baptism day. Be prepared for the unexpected — they may be nervous, excited, resistant, and so on. This is new and (assuming their family is not, or newly, participating in the parish) unfamiliar to them, which means it may be scary. Don't rush them, and if at any time during the Rite itself you sense the need to pause and give that child and their parents time to talk, cry, breathe, and so on, don't hesitate to do so. It happens. The most important thing will be how you respond, when it does. Here, pastoral care takes precedent.

Q. I have parents asking to baptize their child who's much older (ages 7 or 8 and up). How do I handle Baptism preparation for children past the age of reason?

A. In short, a child who has reached the age of reason (also called "catechetical age" or "age of discretion") goes through an adaptation of the OCIA (Order of Christian Initiation of Adults). The OCIA is *the* pathway for children "who have attained the use of reason and are of catechetical age." [141] Because these children are old enough to profess personal faith (as distinct from their parents professing it on their behalf) and are thus considered "adult" not in maturity but in capacity, they receive all three Sacraments of Initiation (Baptism, Confirmation, and Eucharist) preferably at the Easter Vigil. Do remember that at this point, a child's desire (or lack of) affects the validity of the sacrament. We can't baptize a child at this age who really doesn't want to be baptized. They must come freely ("freely" in the sense of "absent of any coercion").

The most important thing to remember here is that your "student" is still the whole family — there are reasons why this child or family hasn't requested Baptism until now. The Christian initiation process is well-equipped to address those reasons and lead the entire family (if willing) into a journey of ongoing conversion. In today's culture, it's likely that older children seeking Baptism will become the "rule" rather than the exception. In fact, you may be watching it happen in real time! Depending on the size of your parish or what's on your own plate, that may also feel that it is a huge ministry expenditure you don't have time to put together. For what it's worth, remember that, in time, some of those offerings will fade or merge. An OCIA done well is also an excellent way to reinvigorate the evangelization of your parish. Don't be afraid to start small and offer only what you can reasonably do, but also keep in mind that you are forging a new path for a very different destination. Your future parish will thank you later for the seeds you are planting now!

RESOURCE RECOMMENDATION

We enthusiastically recommend the book *Guide to Adapting the RCIA for Children* by Rita Burns Sensemen. You'll learn about various models and methods you can use to help a child and their family move through an adapted OCIA process, many of which take advantage of things you're already doing — religious education programs, youth ministry, Catholic schools, and so on. She also provides helpful questions to ask when you're meeting with a child and their parents, as well as guidance for discernment in how to choose the best approach for that child based on the resources your parish currently has.

FIELD NOTES—from Rita Burns Sensemen

"... [Y]ou may be thinking the process of initiation for children is too complicated, takes too much work, and takes too much time. Wouldn't it be easier just to baptize the children and let them join their peers in the regular religious education program or Catholic school? Why do we have different models of initiation for different children? Kids are kids. Why not treat them all the same? It's true: kids are kids. And each one is beautifully different. Furthermore, the Church has different pathways of initiation depending upon the age and circumstances of the children. On the other hand, those different pathways lead children to the same place — the Paschal Mystery. For that's what the Sacraments of Initiation do: They lead us into the mystery of Christ, whether we are adults or children." [142]

Q. How should I work with children who are past the age of reason, but have cognitive disabilities or diverse learning needs?

A. Because these kids think differently from their typically developing peers, even though *chronologically* they may be at the age the Church would consider the age of reason, *developmentally* it is important here to individually discern whether or not this person is a candidate for infant Baptism or for coming into the Church through the OCIA route. This is especially important if they're in that grey zone of seven or eight years old. The National Catholic Partnership on Disability (NCPD) works with the U.S. bishops to provide guidelines for sacramental preparation, when working with persons with disabilities. These are excellent guidelines for us to turn to when we have questions about administering sacraments!

Additionally, keep in mind the unique struggles that the parents of these children have probably encountered during the years. Attune to their pastoral needs and make an extra effort to listen to their story and affirm that they (and their child) belong in your parish community.

RESOURCE RECOMMENDATION

United States Conference of Catholic Bishops, *Guidelines for the Celebration of Sacraments with Persons with Disabilities:* https://www.usccb.org/committees/divine-worship/policies/guidelines-sacraments-persons-with-disabilities.

The *Catechetical Institute* will have an upcoming track on *Franciscan At Home* for "Catechesis for Persons with Disabilities" and already has a workshop of the same title.

Saint Margaret of Castello, patron of persons with disabilities, pray for us.

Q. What happens if a parent in my baptismal preparation process loses a child to miscarriage, stillbirth, or infant loss? How should I handle this situation?

A. First, give the gift of presence and of words. In any situation involving death, grief, or loss, we often feel awkward or uncomfortable ("I don't know what to say!"). Since we don't want to make things worse, we may err on the side of not saying anything at all. We'd urge you to do otherwise. This is a place where our love for life at all stages should be compassionate and vocal. No matter how far along, these parents just lost a baby. Their flesh and blood. Their child died. Don't be afraid to name their loss, so they have permission to grieve properly. "I am so sorry about the loss of your baby," or similar words. If you know other parents within your parish community who have walked this road, consider inviting them to accompany this family. If you are blessed to have a bereavement ministry team, this is the time to call upon them.

Second, give the gift of practical guidance and help. Things move quickly, and parents are often forced to make rushed choices — in the middle of an already devastating and traumatic situation — without knowing all their options. Familiarize yourself with this process, as well as with local or national resources. Your hospital or diocese may already have a ministry designed to support parents through these situations.

Finally, offer the comfort and assurance of sound theological teaching and pastoral guidance. The death of a child — especially in miscarriage or stillbirth when the baby has died before being baptized — can be fraught with confusion and misunderstandings (for example, "limbo," salvation concerns, and so on). Many of the faithful are unaware that situations involving miscarriage or stillbirth can be treated the same as any other child who dies before Baptism, even if the body of the infant is not present. The "Prayers after Death" and other "Related Rites and Prayers" in the Order of Christian Funerals (OCF) Part I may be used in the home or hospital shortly after the death of the child, with wording adapted to the circumstances. The parents can also greatly benefit from the opportunity to name their child. Additionally, the family can still be accompanied through funeral rites. As noted in OCF, "Funeral rites may be celebrated for children whose parents intended them to be baptized, but who died before Baptism. In these celebrations, the Christian community entrusts the child to God's all-embracing love and finds strength in this love and in Jesus' affirmation that the Kingdom of God belongs to little children." [143]

FROM THE CATECHISM

"As regards *children who have died without Baptism*, the Church can only entrust them to the mercy of God, as she does in her funeral rites for them. Indeed, the great mercy of God who desires that all men should be saved and Jesus' tenderness toward children which caused Him to say: 'Let them come to me, do not hinder them' allow us to hope that there is a way of salvation for children who have died without Baptism. All the more urgent is the Church's call not to prevent little children coming to Christ through the gift of holy Baptism." [144]

RESOURCE RECOMMENDATION

Red Bird Ministries is a Catholic organization devoted to systematically guiding individuals and couples through the complexity and trauma of any stage of child loss, and it can be a great place to begin familiarizing yourself with available resources (www.redbird.love). Recognize that grief is ongoing and be committed to walking with these parents not only now, but also in the months and years to come.

Mary, Mother of the crucified Christ, pray for all grieving parents, and for their families.

Q. My parish is extremely small. It's just me and a handful of families. What do I do?

A. If you're in a parish where you're the parish catechetical leader, secretary, maintenance figure, judge, jury, and executioner, please know you're not alone, even if you are literally alone! On the one hand, sometimes you wish you could focus on just one ministry for any amount of time. You don't have resources to spend on ideas that aren't productive, especially since you will have statistically fewer Baptisms and you want those opportunities to be fruitful.

On the other hand, you also have the greatest advantage when it comes to baptismal preparation because YOU KNOW EVERYONE IN THE ENTIRE PARISH. When someone comes to have their child baptized, you are the best person in the world to get them connected to the right people and places. Think of yourself like the parish "matchmaker" — connect them to parish families who would be thrilled to help them (and you), provided you ask. The benefit of an approach that is inspired by the rite, proclamation of the *kerygma*, and focused on community is that you don't need a lot of bells and whistles to do it.

No matter what, remember Jesus sees you and your labor. Perhaps more than others, you're wearing an unusually large number of hats. Focus on the person in front of you and don't be tempted by flashy programs, knowing that the best ministry happens when you simply notice what the Holy Spirit is doing in another person's heart and guide that person toward Jesus. Last, but not least, make sure that someone is taking care of *you*, too, whether it's your pastor or someone else who can be present for you when you need a shoulder to cry on, someone to commiserate with, or some words of encouragement. Without exception, find a prayer warrior and share your challenges and your schedule. (If you can't find that person right away, remember that, we're here for you, cheering you on, and praying for you).

RESOURCE RECOMMENDATION

If you don't currently have a mentor, but would like one, consider requesting an individual mentor through the *Catechetical Institute* on *Franciscan At Home* workshops (www.franciscanathome.com) or joining the *International Guild for Catechists and Leaders* (www.franciscanathome.com/guild). Either option will connect you with other catechetical leaders across the globe, for guidance, solidarity, and collaboration!

Q. My parish is huge. How do I apply these principles in a very large parish?

A. If you're in a large parish ripe with resources but still see opportunity for improvement in your baptismal preparation, we'd offer a few suggestions. You likely have several staff members, a larger pool of volunteer catechists, and a more diverse parish overall — this is an incredible asset that allows you to draw from multiple options when connecting families preparing for Baptism with others from the parish community. Though tempting, don't neglect individual interviews with parents. Hundreds of Baptisms may feel overwhelming, but enlist help instead of cutting corners. Train your staff and/or volunteers in the art of asking good questions and empathic listening, then set them loose. Large numbers of Baptisms can also be a strength — consider pooling parents together in small groups or cohorts, assign them a faithful mentor, and send them on their journey. Your field is larger, but that also allows you to begin new cohorts frequently and quickly (for example, a new intake group could start every month). These families can also celebrate the baptismal liturgy together.

One of the liabilities of working in a large parish is that sometimes you can get bogged down in administrative details and parish red tape, so you don't get to see the direct, tangible fruit of your ministry as often. This can tempt you toward discouragement. To this end:

1. *Stay "in the trenches" in at least one area of ministry.* Handle some of the interviews or run a group. Don't forget the faces, names, and stories of those who are on the outermost edges. There is great joy in being reminded that you are actively participating in bringing souls to Jesus.

2. *Don't forget that you are not only just administering, but also ministering to those on your staff and leadership team.* Get to know their faces, names, and stories — personally and spiritually. There is great joy (and necessity) in accompanying leaders toward sainthood, as they partner with you in ministry.

3. *Make sure you have someone to minister to you, as well.* It might be a pastor or another spiritual director or mentor. Don't buy into the

lie that you're a channel and not a reservoir. You need a place to go for encouragement and solidarity, where you can get "filled up" to serve out of generosity, not need.

In short, it sometimes takes more time to turn a bigger ship, but you can also take more people along for the ride. You'll have statistically more Baptism opportunities than a smaller parish. This means that once you start making disciples out of these families, you'll gain some serious ministry momentum for the next generation of the Church.

RESOURCE RECOMMENDATION

If you don't currently have a mentor, but would like one, consider requesting an individual mentor through the *Catechetical Institute* on *Franciscan At Home* workshops (www.franciscanathome.com) or joining the *International Guild for Catechists and Leaders* (www.franciscanathome.com/guild). Either option will connect you with other catechetical leaders across the globe, for guidance, solidarity, and collaboration!

Q. We have a small (meaning nonexistent) budget. Does this work with limited finances?

A. You don't have money. But remember — you can't buy salvation, disciples, saints, or God's love. We shouldn't lose hope when we lack the financial resources of the parish down the road. Jesus and His disciples were frequently without "enough" money — you remember the multiplication of loaves from the *Gospel of St. John*, Chapter 6, we quote when we are defending the Eucharist? There are simple and powerful steps to help:

- *Employ your prayer team.* Fasting and prayer can and will move mountains. If choosing between your budget multiplied tenfold or ten people in Adoration for your ministry, take ten people in Adoration every time. Remember to be in regular contact with your intercessors, such as the cloistered, sick, or home-bound.

- *Hospitality is a charism, not an expense.* You don't need expensive catering to create a warm environment. A few cheap candles and decent pot of coffee can go a long way.

- *A listening ear is priceless.* People spend a great deal on therapy. You aren't a therapist (don't try to be), but you *can* create a safe place for someone else's story to unfold. Your most valuable assets are an empathic ear and an open heart. Use them both. Frequently.

- *The most effective resources are free.* Scripture, the *Catechism*, and the baptismal rite are amazing tools. Use them. The Church never *expects* you to need anything else.

At the risk of sounding cavalier, God has lots of money — all of it, in fact — and He holds nothing back for what is necessary in His work. If you feel your finances are limited, it may mean you don't need them for the ministry under your care. Look at what you have, then look at Him and say, "Thank you for giving me all I need." You will do amazing things, money or not.

Saint Nicholas, protector of the poor, pray for us.

Saint Matthew, patron of financial matters, pray for us.

Ministering in Special Situations

Q. We're in a big city. How do we minister to the unique urban context of our people?

A. You'd think a large metropolitan area would provide prime real estate for community and connection, but "... paradoxically it not rarely becomes the place of greatest solitude, disappointment, and distrust . . ." [145] It's far easier to isolate ourselves when we're one face in a million. As a light in a dark place, your parish could bring families together in a loving, human, fraternal way, "... capable of offering community contexts of faith in which, by overcoming anonymity, the value of each person is recognized and everyone is offered the balm of Paschal faith in order to soothe the injury." [146] As you plan your baptismal preparation, ask for the Holy Spirit's creativity to help you "... imagine innovative spaces and possibilities for prayer and communion which are more attractive and meaningful for city dwellers." [147] Parents seeking Baptism aren't just learning the faith together, they're learning how to be Catholic parents together, and that's best done in community.

Q. Our diocese/parish is rural and families live far from the parish and each other. How do we meet these unique needs?

A. In the past, rural families were more insulated from modernity, but increased globalization and digitization pose new threats for "communities of the countryside." [148] Many smaller family farms have been sold, absorbed, or are renting land to larger operations, leaving families to seek work and commute to suburban or metropolitan areas. On the plus side, many rural parishes still maintain an integrated sense of community. This can be both good and bad. The benefit? You may be working with a close-knit group of parishioners, who embrace their unique communal identity. The drawback? The lack of evangelization in Catholic culture at large can lead to an isolated community that doesn't reach out.

In these cases, remember that rural parishes have a strong sense of personal ownership in the work of their parish. Many of them would not exist were it not for the dedicated volunteer hours of the parishioners. Rural communities aren't afraid of work. Now, it needs to be redirected to the missionary vision of the early Church. Proclaiming the *kerygma* to your own people is crucial to harness the momentum of the parish. After all, many of them have been functioning like staff or leadership for years — on no pay. Help them see the purpose. They'll do the work.

Saint Joseph, patron of workers, pray for us.

Saint Isidore, patron saint of farmers, pray for us and our rural families.

P.S. Though they have their own strengths and limitations, challenges of a rural parish are similar to small parishes or parishes with limited finances. If that's true for yours, refer to those sections, as well. We also recommend the *Catechetical Institute's* workshop "Rural Youth Ministry" for ideas that are also applicable for sacramental preparation.

Q. How do I offer effective baptismal preparation in a multicultural/multiethnic setting?

A. Consider Paul's missionary journey. One of his most effective techniques was equipping a native of the culture to continue ministry, once he moved on. We may find ourselves *receiving* people from multiple cultures, but the Spirit is the same. Our Church is one without borders, so it's important that our own catechesis reflects this attitude. "Where it is possible, offering catechesis that takes into account the ways and understanding and practicing the faith typical of the countries of origin constitutes a valuable support for the Christian life of migrants, above all for the first generation. Great importance is attached to the use of the mother tongue, because it is the first form of expression of their identity." [149] For us, this means we do our best to organize, "catechetical programs for Christian initiation and ongoing formation, conducted in the language and according to the traditions of the churches of origin." [150]

This might be daunting for any of us to achieve if we don't speak the language or understand the traditions and customs from their land of origin. But as we've said many times before, you're not supposed to do this on your own. If we want to effectively minister in multicultural situations, we need to look within those cultures, seeking disciples and catechists who can help bridge the gap from their own side. These individuals can inform us of needs we may have previously been unaware of, helping our catechesis "to be particularly attentive in the first place to *getting to know* the people with whom it maintains a sincere and patient dialogue, and is to seek to *examine* such cultures in the light of the Gospel" [151] In complement with our knowledge of Church teaching, we benefit here from taking the role of student.

Ultimately, don't forget that the goal is to have a unified parish — not just one that "offers (insert language here)-speaking" Mass. Not one where everyone looks the same. Not one where each individual culture exists isolated from each other. One Body, because we have One Head, Jesus.[152] We want our cultures to begin to relate to each other openly and naturally. And we lead from the front. By naturally and openly working with catechists from multiple cultures, you model the very process by which the Church moves forward. Finally, remember that many of your parish families will have maintained at least a whisper of the ethnic way of handing on the faith often lost in western cultures — whether they realize it or not, their faith is likely deeply embedded into their homes and lives. Point this out to them and reawaken a domestic church that may lay dormant because of assimilation. In the long run, these families may be the very ones who minister *to you.*

Saint Martin de Porres, pray for us.

Our Lady of Guadalupe, pray for us.

Ministering in Special Situations

Appendix:

Helpful Tools, Programs, and Resources

A TOOL IS JUST THAT — A TOOL. BUT THE RIGHT TOOL, when sharp, can make your job a lot easier. Although no program by itself is sufficient for a truly robust baptismal preparation process (a textbook isn't a great wingman to help families meet others in their community), the right resource in the hands of the right person is a great beginning. In the spirit of faithful creativity, these are a few resources we've found helpful (though there are probably several others not listed here). Of course, remember that God has already given you and your parish all you need to minister to your community — no "program" required!

The *Catechetical Institute's* website, *Fraciscan at Home*, through Franciscan University of Steubenville,

https://franciscanathome.com/

The *Catechetical Institute*'s workshop:

The Sacrament of Baptism,

This online workshop is a comprehensive yet accessible study of the Sacrament of Baptism. It can be completed at your own pace, on your own time, or you could take your catechists through it as a group. There's also an option to request a mentor, who will guide you through the workshop (highly recommended, because it is close to having someone in the field bring you a cup of coffee and hash out ministry with you!)

Association for Catechumenal Ministry,

OCIA Catechist's Manual,

https://acmrcia.org/resources/

Bishop Robert Barron's Word On Fire,

Pivotal Players Series On Ignatius of Loyola,

https://www.wofdigital.org/new-the-pivotal-players-bartolome-de-las-casas-st-ignatius-of-loyola

Ascension Press,

Belonging: Baptism in the Family of God*,

This bilingual resource places huge emphasis on winning over the hearts of the parents, helping them encounter Christ and reminding them that they (not just their baby) are loved by God. The videos are brief but poignant, and the workbooks ask great questions bridging the material and the spiritual. This particular program is robust and does a lot of the heavy lifting for a catechetical leader, making it a great support for an overworked catechetical leader. That said, avoid the temptation of leaning on it too heavily — it (like any program) can't replace you and your community!

Catherine of Sienna Institute,

Great Story of Jesus,

https://learning.siena.org/product/ananias-who-do-you-say-that-i-am-the-great-story-of-jesus-in-nine-acts/

Diocese of Phoenix,

A Catechumenal Approach to Infant Baptism,

http://dphx.org/wp-content/uploads/2016/01/A-Catechumenal-Approach-to-Infant-Baptism.pdf

Our Sunday Visitor,

Catholic Parent Know-How: Preparing Your Child for Baptism and How to Be a Godparent*,

Super brief but practical guides not only for the Sacrament of Baptism (though it does that and does it well), but also to what it might look like to live out those baptismal promises in simple ways during the next several years. Not intimidating and a great way to introduce parents to the idea of forming their domestic church and godparents to their responsibilities for helping this child grow in faith.

TAN Books,

First Steps in Your Journey of Faith and Parish Life: A Baby Journal from Baptism to First Reconciliation,

A baby book with a refreshing spiritual focus that lasts from birth and Baptism all the way to a child's First Communion. It's simple — just enough prompts to remember highlights and milestones, but not overwhelming. It also seamlessly integrates natural and spiritual development. You'll find a place for baby's footprints and birth facts right across from a page to record memories from the Baptism. This could make an excellent gift from the parish for families who've baptized a child.

Intentional Catholic Parenting (ICP),

Tools for Raising Disciples with Kim Cameron-Smith,

This ministry website is a wealth of resources for Catholic parents, and one of the few that is truly principle-based in its approach. Beginning with the assumption that parents are the primary and most powerful catechists for their children, the mission of ICP is to give Catholic parents confidence and tools needed for the journey of raising disciples by focusing on two core areas: 1) nurturing the parent-child connection and 2) building a radiant home faith culture. Through podcasts, blog articles, e-newsletters, and a lovely resource page, ICP guides parents with grace, nuance, encouragement, and faithfulness!

Interior Kingdom,

A Catholic parenting program that teaches emotional regulation to the whole family,

Guided by our Catholic faith while incorporating the best of contemporary psychology, this unique, new apostolate helps Catholic parents practically work through the big feelings that come with raising little humans. Featuring beautiful, original artwork and "Kingdom of Heaven" language inspired by Teresa of Avila's book, *The Interior Castle*, this program teaches parents and children how to navigate emotional landscapes and find their way back to King Jesus. An excellent option especially for families who baptized children years ago — this program works well for toddlers all the way through teenagers!

National Catholic Partnership on Disability (NCPD),

www.ncpd.org

Liturgical Press,

The Order of Baptism for Children, 2020 edition,

https://litpress.org/Products/6509/The-Order-of-Baptism-of-Children

Our Sunday Visitor,

Parent Letters from Your Parish*,

Seven chronological packets designed to be distributed at six-month intervals, starting right after Baptism and continuing through the child's third birthday. The letter includes age-appropriate parenting strategies and helpful advice. Plus, you get seven small gifts — one to send along with each letter. Even the mailing envelopes are included!

Greg and Lisa Popcak,

Parenting Your Kids with Grace: Birth to Age 10,

Written by a family therapist (Dr. Greg Popcak) and his wife Lisa, both of whom are experienced Catholic parents, this book is an excellent resource for parents, as they navigate their new vocation. It combines solid parenting principles with up-to-date research to guide parents through each stage of child development. We love it, because it explicitly addresses what it means not only to be a parent who happens to be Catholic, but also to parent as a Catholic. A great resource to keep in your library for parents in your parish!

Sister Hyacinthe DeFos du Rau, OP,

Preparing for Your Child's Baptism,

A brief but powerful little booklet that explains what the sacrament is all about and what it means for a parent and their child. Sister Hyacinthe offers practical suggestions and activities to follow during the time of preparation and on the day of the Baptism itself to support their child in prayer together with all the family.

Red Bird Ministries,

www.redbird.love

Loyola Press,

Springs of Faith,*

A bilingual, multifaceted, primarily digital program that aims to help people become lifelong followers of Christ. Its model is also inspired by the catechumenate: The "Discover" phase meets parents where they're at with informal faith-sharing gatherings. The "Encounter" phase includes preparation for the Sacrament of Baptism itself. The "Share" phase lays the foundation for building a home of faith (domestic church) with both post-baptismal sessions AND guidance for hosting baby-and-me-style parent groups within your parish. A fantastic resource either comprehensively, or a la carte.

Dynamic Catholic,

Starting Point,

This is another program with brief, poignant videos and workbooks that ask great questions, both to parents and to godparents. We really like the *Parent's Journal for Dreaming,* as well as the follow-up focus — not only on Baptism preparation, but also on the parenting journey and the kinds of skills and support needed for Catholic parents.

Thomistic Institute,

https://thomisticinstitute.org/

United States Conference of Catholic Bishops,

Guidelines for the Celebration of Sacraments with Persons with Disabilities,

https://www.usccb.org/committees/divine-worship/policies/guidelines-sacraments-persons-with-disabilities

Pflaum Publishing Group,

Welcoming God's Children: Baptism Connection — Family Packet,

A bunch of resources you can use to foster connection between the parish and the family of a recently baptized child. Again, resources don't replace the parish community, but they can be the icing on the proverbial cake. Each packet contains:

- *Baptism Beginnings: A Parent's Guide to Baptism.* A helpful little booklet.

- *You Are My Godchild: A Sponsor's Journal* (Two copies). Faithful journaling exercises, Bible verses, prayers, and devotions for the sponsor to complete and hold on to as a keepsake until that child's First Communion.

- *My First Bible Storybook* This colorfully-illustrated collection of 12 beloved Bible stories is written for parents to read to children ages 1–3.

- *My First Year of Faith* This calendar marks the physical and spiritual development of the newly baptized child through the first year of his/her life. Stickers are included to track faith and growth milestones.

- **Baptism Birthday Cards** (Set of six) These cards are designed to be given by the Godparent (or by a parish worker) on their godchild's baptismal anniversary through age 6.

- **Child's Baptism Certificate.**

- **Sponsor's Baptism Certificate** (Two copies).

FORMED*,

https://formed.org/

If your parish has a subscription to Formed, this can be a great source for materials in both English and Spanish. But there is a caveat: you *must* have actual people from the parish community facilitating discussions. The community piece must be present in some way to make this complete! A few recommendations:

- The Search. A *kerygmatic* resource that can be powerful for middle school through adult. Using the videos wisely with small group discussion afterward could prove very rich!

- The Catholic Parent. A resource much loved by families with small children. Excellent points and humor that can be appreciated!

- Catholic Mom's Summit. A large collection of videos on all kinds of felt needs relevant for mothers.

Again, used with discretion and facilitation, Formed could be a way of fostering community for those who've already baptized babies. Formed also frequently adds new resources that engage different groups according to need, so check back often.

*Also available in Spanish

Bibliography

Scripture citations are from the *Revised Standard Version Catholic Edition*, unless noted otherwise.

Vatican documents can be found at https://www.vatican.va/content/vatican/en.html.

Augustine, *First Catechetical Instruction*, trans. Rev. Joseph P Christopher. Newman Press, 1946.

Benedict XVI's "Address to Participants in the Plenary Assembly of the Pontifical Council for the Family" on the theme "Grandparents: Their Witness and Presence in the Family," May 13, 2006.

St. Bernard of Clairvaux, *Commentary on the Song of Songs I*, trans. Killian Walsh. Cistercian Publications, 1971.

Cambridge Dictionary. https://dictionary.cambridge.org/us/dictionary/english/field-manual#.

Carroll, Lewis, *Alice's Adventures in Wonderland,* in *The Annotated Alice,* Clarkson N. Potter, Inc., 1960.

Corbitt, Sonja, *Exalted: How the Power of the Magnificat can Transform Us.* Ave Maria Press, 2019.

Ferrer, St. Vincent, "Sermon on the Baptism of Jesus Matthew 3:14." https://www.svfsermons.org/A248_Baptism%20of%20Jesus.htm.

Francis, "Address at the Meeting of Families in Santiago de Cuba," September 22, 2015.

Francis, Apostolic Exhortation "On the Proclamation of the Gospel in Today's World," *Evangelii gaudium,* November 13, 2013.

Francis, Encyclical Letter "On Faith," *Lumen fidei,* June 29, 2013.

Francis, Post-Synodal Apostolic Exhortation "On Love in the Family," *Amoris laetitia,* March 19, 2016.

Francis de Sales, *Treatise on the Love of God*, trans. H.B. Mackey. London: Burns Oates & Washbourne, 1884.

Congregation for the Clergy, *General Directory for Catechesis,* August 11, 1997.

Gregory of Nazianzus, *Oratio* 40, 3–4: *PG* 36, 361C.

Heath, Dan, *Upstream: The Quest to Solve Problems Before They Matter.* Avid Reader Press, 2020.

International Council for Catechesis, *Adult Catechesis in the Christian Community*, 1990.

John Paul II, "Homily of the Holy Father During Mass with Young People," April 26, 1997.

John Paul II, "The Seafarer's Prayer," adapted from concluding prayer in his Post-Synodal Apostolic Exhortation "On Jesus Christ and the Peoples of Oceania: Walking His Way, Telling His Truth, Living His Life," *Ecclesia in Oceania,* November 22, 2001.

John Paul II, 15th World Youth Day Vigil of Prayer Address, August 19, 2000.

John Paul II, Apostolic Exhortation "On Catechesis in Our Time," *Catechesi tradendae,* October 16, 1979.

John Paul II, Apostolic Letter "At the Close of the Great Jubilee of the Year 2000," *Novo millennio ineunte*, January 6, 2001.

Catechism of the Catholic Church, 2nd ed. Washington, DC: United States Catholic Conference, 2011.

John XXIII, *Address on the Opening of the Second Vatican Ecumenical Council*, October 11, 1962.

Keimig, William, *The Sower* (now *Catechetical Review*), "RCIA: Questions, Answers, Issues and Advice," Issue #32.3, July–September 2011. Accessed 1/2/2025, https://franciscanathome.com/the-catechetical-review/articles/rcia-questions-answers-issues-and-advice.

Lewis, C. S., *Mere Christianity*. London: Harper Collins, 2001.

Merriam Webster Dictionary. Accessed November 19, 2024. https://www.merriam-webster.com/dictionary/incorporate#:~text=transitive%20verb-,1,business)%20into%20a%20legal%20corporation.

Order of Baptism of Children, 2nd Edition, The Liturgical Press, 2020.

Order of Christian Funerals, in *The Rites of the Catholic Church,* Vol. 1, The Liturgical Press, 1990.

Paul VI, Apostolic Exhortation, "Evangelization in the Modern World," *Evangelii nuntiandi*, December 8, 1975.

Philippe, Jacques, *In the School of the Holy Spirit*. Scepter Publishers, Inc., 2007.

Pontifical Council for the Promotion of the New Evangelization, *Directory for Catechesis*. March 23, 2020.

Association for Catechumenal Ministry, *OCIA Catechist's Manual*. https://acmocia.org/resources/

Order of Christian Initiation of Adults: Study Edition. Liturgical Training Publications, 2024.

Rite of Matrimony, in *The Rites of the Catholic Church*, Vol. 1, The Liturgical Press, 1990.

Sacred Congregation for the Doctrine of the Faith, "Instruction on Infant Baptism," *Pastoralis actio*, October 20, 1980.

Second Vatican Council, Dogmatic Constitution "On the Church," *Lumen gentium*, November 21, 1964.

Second Vatican Council, Pastoral Constitution "On the Church in the Modern World," *Gaudium et spes*, December 7, 1965.

Sensemen, Rita Burns, *Guide to Adapting the RCIA for Children*. Liturgy Training Publications, 2017.

Tertullian, *On Baptism*. https://www.churchfathers.org/necessity-of-baptism.

The Order of Christian Funerals, in *The Rites of the Catholic Church,* Vol. 1, The Liturgical Press, 1990.

White, Joseph, Workshop "Keeping Kids Catholic," Franciscan University of Steubenville's St. John Bosco Conference, 2021.

Zoom interview between Dr. Martha Drennan and Michael and Jacqueline Van Hemert on May 11, 2021.

Zoom interview between Margaret Wickware and Michael and Jacqueline Van Hemert, May 14, 2021.

Zoom interview between Sister Hyacinthe DeFos du Rau, OP and Michael and Jacqueline Van Hemert, June 7, 2021.

Zoom interview with Carol Ann Harnett and Michael and Jacqueline Van Hemert, April 29, 2021.

Endnotes

[1] *Matthew* 28:19–20.

[2] This conviction is powerfully presented in *The Soul of the Apostolate* by Jean Baptiste-Chautard. Originally written for priests, but very relevant for anyone serving in a parish apostolate, the work as a whole is a reminder that the secret to bearing spiritual fruit is that we only transmit spiritual life when we have been open to receive it from Christ ourselves.

[3] If you haven't read St. Augustine; *First Catechetical Instruction*, we think you'd find it very enjoyable. On Deogratias and his struggles, see 1; 14-23.

[4] See *John* 8:12.

[5] C. S. Lewis, *Mere Christianity*, 45–46.

[6] St. John XXIII, Address on the Opening of the Second Vatican Ecumenical Council.

Endnotes

[7] Pontifical Council for the Promotion of the New Evangelization, *Directory for Catechesis* (DC) 64.

[8] *DC* 63.

[9] *DC* 63.

[10] Congregation for the Clergy, *General Directory for Catechesis* 59.

[11] *Isaiah* 62:4.

[12] *Luke* 1:35.

[13] See *Matthew* 13:1–23.

[14] If you found this fruitful or wish to learn more about this ancient practice of the Church of praying with Scripture, we recommend the *Catechetical Institute's* workshop. "Praying with Scripture: Lectio Divina."

[15] *Psalm* 65:9–13.

[16] Sts. Bernard of Clairvaux, *On the Song of Songs,* 18: 3, 5.

[17] See *Matthew* 3:13–17; *Mark* 1:9–11; *Luke* 3:21–22.

[18] See St. Vincent Ferrer, "Sermon on the Baptism of Jesus Matthew 3:14," quoting St. Bede's homily, "The Son of God comes to be baptized by a man in the water of the Jordan, He Who was pure of all uncleanness, that washing the filth of all our sins, He might sanctify the flowing of the waters." https://www.svfsermons.org/A248_Baptism%20of%20Jesus.htm.

[19] *John* 1:23; cf. *Isaiah* 40:3

[20] St. Gregory of Nazianzus, *Oratio* 40, 3–4: *PG* 36, 361C.

[21] Sonja Corbitt, *Exalted: How the Power of the Magnificat can Transform Us*, Notre Dame, IN: Ave Maria Press, 2019, 6.

[22] Those who are parents via the gift of adoption may not physcially give birth, but they walk through a very unique and often agonizing labor of their own.

[23] See Second Vatican Council, *Lumen gentium* 11; *Catechism of the Catholic Church* 1655–1658.

[24] *CCC* 1214; cf. *Romans* 6:4; *Colossians* 2:12.

[25] St. John Paul II, "15th World Youth Day Vigil of Prayer Address" 5.

[26] *Alice in Wonderland*, in *The Annotated Alice*, NY: Clarkson N Potter, 1960, 88.

[27] *CCC* 1.

[28] *Rite of Matrimony*, 26.

[29] *CCC* 1253.

[30] *CCC* 1818, 1820

[31] Zoom Interview between Sister Hyacinthe Defos du Rau, OP and Michael and Jacqueline Van Hemert on June 7, 2021.

[32] St. Vincent Ferrer, "Sermon on the Baptism of Jesus." https://www.svfsermons.org/A248_Baptism%20of%20Jesus.htm.

[33] Refers to the Magisterium, or the official teaching authority of the Church; see CCC 85–87.

[34] *CCC* 1213.

[35] *CCC* 1214.

[36] *CCC* 1225; cf. *John* 19:34; *1 John* 5:6–8.

[37] *CCC* 1220.

[38] *CCC* 1218; cf. *Genesis* 1:2.

[39] *CCC* 1219; cf. 1 *Peter* 3:20.

[40] *CCC* 1221.

[41] *Romans* 6:3–4.

[42] St. Ambrose, *De sacr.* 2, 2, 6: PL 16, 444; cf. *John* 3:5, quoted in *CCC* 1225.

[43] *1 Peter* 5:8.

[44] *CCC* 1237.

[45] See *Hebrews* 11:19.

[46] *Isaiah* 55:1 (New American Bible Revised Edition translation).

[47] *CCC* 1250.

[48] Sacred Congregation for the Doctrine of the Faith, *Instruction on Infant Baptism, Pastoralis actio* 14.

[49] *Pastoralis actio* 14.

[50] *Pastoralis actio* 2.

[51] *Pastoralis actio* 7.

[52] Second Vatican Council's Pastoral Constitution "On the Church in the Modern World," *Gaudium et spes* 50; *CCC* 1251.

[53] *Pastoralis actio* 26, quoting *1 John* 4:10.

[54] *Titus* 3:5.

[55] See *CCC* 1213.

[56] See *CCC* 1213 and 1267.

[57] *Merriam Webster Dictionary*.

[58] St. Vincent Ferrer, "Sermon on the Baptism of Jesus."

[59] *CCC* 1231.

[60] *CCC* 1253; Cf. *Mark* 16:16.

[61] *CCC* 1254.

[62] *CCC* 1255; Cf. *CIC*, can. 872-874.

[63] *CCC* 1255.

[64] *1 Peter* 2:2.

[65] *CCC* 1270.

[66] Zoom interview between Dr. Martha Drennan and Michael and Jacqueline Van Hemert on May 11, 2021.

[67] *RCIA Catechist's Manual*, Introduction, Section 5, 34.

[68] *RCIA Catechist's Manual*, Introduction Section 5, 34.

[69] *RCIA Catechist's Manual*, Introduction Section 5, 34–35.

[70] *The Order of Baptism of Children.*

[71] *DC* 95–96.

[72] *DC* 76.

[73] *DC* 80.

[74] *DC* 80.

[75] *CCC* 1251; Cf. *LG* 11; 41; *GS* 48; *CIC*, can. 868.

[76] See *Matthew* 19:14.

[77] *CCC* 1253.

[78] *Pastoralis actio* 28.

[79] Zoom interview between Margaret Wickware and Michael and Jacqueline Van Hemert on May 14, 2021.

[80] Tertullian, *On Baptism*, Chapter 1.

[81] For more on primary prevention, see Upstream: *The Quest to Solve Problems Before They Matter* by Dan Heath.

[82] *DC* 116d.

[83] *DC* 229.

[84] *DC* 232c.

[85] *DC* 30, cf. Gregory of Nyssa in his *Oratio catechetica*, 37: Gregorii Nysseni Opera 3/4 97–98 (PG 45:97) wrote: "In his manifestation

God joined Himself to mortal nature so that through participation in divinity humanity could be divinized together with Him." Generally, the Christian West has preferred the language of salvation, whereas the Christian East has preferred the language of divinization. But they're both correct. In fact, they're complementary. One emphasizes what we are saved from, the other what we are saved for; cf. *2 Peter* 1:4.

[86] Pope Francis, Apostolic Exhortation "On the Proclamation of the Gospel in Today's World," *Evangelii gaudium* 164.

[87] *DC* 57–60.

[88] *Evangelii gaudium* 34.

[89] *Evangelii gaudium* 63.

[90] See *Acts* 8:26–40, where Philip evangelizes the Ethiopian eunuch.

[91] *DC* 61; cf. St. John Paul II, Apostolic Exhortation "On Catechesis in Our Time," *Catechesi tradendae* 44.

[92] This was a point helpfully made by Joseph White in a workshop "Keeping Kids Catholic," given at Franciscan University of Steubenville's St. John Bosco Conference, 2021.

[93] *DC* 232c.

[94] *DC* 64e and 64f.

[95] *DC* 131.

[96] *DC* 64f.

[97] St. John Paul II, "Homily of the Holy Father During Mass with Young People," April 26, 1997.

[98] A style of children's gamebook, written from a second-person point of view, the reader assuming the role of the protagonist and making decisions that determine main character's actions and thus the plot's outcome.

[99] *Luke* 5:4.

[100] St. John Paul II "At the Close of the Great Jubilee of the Year 2000," *Novo millennio ineunte* 34.

[101] Adapted from St. John Paul II, "The Seafarer's Prayer," concluding prayer in *Ecclesia in Oceania* 53.

[102] *Matthew* 5:6.

[103] *DC* 229.

[104] *DC* 57–60.

[105] *DC* 131.

[106] *John* 15:5.

[107] Father Jacques Philippe, *In the School of the Holy Spirit*, 24.

[108] St. Francis de Sales, *Treatise on the Love of God*, Book 8, Chapter 11.

[109] *DC* 64, quoting *Evangelii gaudium* 166.

[110] This stage is sometimes referred to as the "Inquiry" stage. But doing so limits the understanding of what this period is about and lessens the importance of it. "Inquiry" suggests that focus needs to be simply on answering their questions. But this misunderstanding can eliminate our critical focus on evangelization during this time!

[111] *Evangelii gaudium* 280.

[112] *Galatians* 4:19 (New American Bible Revised Edition translation).

[113] *Catechesi tradendae* 25.

[114] St. Paul VI, "Evangelization in the Modern World," *Evangelii nuntiandi* 14.

[115] *Evangelii gaudium* 164.

[116] Cf. *John* 4:6–7.

[117] Father Jacques Philippe, *In the School of the Holy Spirit*, 10.

[118] *DC* 135c.

[119]   This is a question they may never have been asked, so give them time to think about it. Some people can't answer this question at all, and that is an answer in itself.

[120]   What is meant by "leads a life of faith" is the "bare minimum" of being an actively practicing Catholic: attending Mass on Sundays and holy days of obligation, receiving the Sacraments of the Eucharist and Reconciliation at least once annually, and contributing to the material needs of the Church.

[121]   Practically, this usually comes up in reference to marriage: to be a godparent, one must either not be married, or if married, be in a recognized Catholic marriage.

[122]   *DC* 125.

[123]   *DC* 125, quoting *RCIA* 43 (11).

[124]   *DC* 125.

[125]   *DC* 125.

[126]   *DC* 125.

[127]   *DC* 125.

[128]   *DC* 234.

[129]   *DC* 230.

[130]   *Matthew* 19:13–14

[131]   Keimig, William, *The Sower*, "RCIA: Questions, Answers, Issues and Advice," Issue 32.3, July–September 2011, originally on pages 34–35 in print edition, emphasis added.

[132]   Pope Francis, "Address at the Meeting of Families in Santiago de Cuba", *L'Osservatore Romano*, September 24, 2015, page 7, as quoted in Pope Francis, "On Love in the Family," *Amoris Laetitia* 7.

[133]   *DC* 239.

[134]   *Mark* 10:16.

[135] Zoom interview with Carol Ann Harnett and Michael and Jacqueline Van Hemert.

[136] We cannot stress this enough. If you aren't currently in this season of life, you may recall the struggles, but you won't feel them in your bones like they do.

[137] International Council for Catechesis, *Adult Catechesis in the Christian Community*, 28.

[138] *DC* 262a.

[139] *DC* 233–235.

[140] *DC* 126; cf. Francis, General Audiences, March 4 and 11, 2015, quoting Benedict XVI's "Address to Participants in the Plenary Assembly of the Pontifical Council for the Family" on the theme "Grandparents: Their Witness and Presence in the Family."

[141] *Order of Christian Initiation of Adults: Study Edition* 252.

[142] Sensemen, Rita Burns, *Guide to Adapting the RCIA for Children*.

[143] *Order of Christian Funerals* 237; see *Matthew* 19:14.

[144] *CCC* 1261, quoting *Mark* 10:14; cf. *1 Timothy* 2:4.

[145] *DC* 328.

[146] *DC* 328.

[147] *Evangelii gaudium* 73.

[148] *DC* 329.

[149] *DC* 275.

[150] *DC* 277.

[151] *DC* 333.

[152] Cf. *Colossians* 1:18.

Endnotes

Who We Are

The *Catechetical Institute* (CI) is a large-scale international outreach of Franciscan University of Steubenville for ministry formation. CI was formally organized in 2015 and publicly launched in 2017 to serve Christ and his Church by forming those entrusted with the formation of others in any situation and ministry role — priests, deacons, religious, parents, parish and school leaders, teachers, catechists, and teams, whether professional or volunteer, from homes to diocesan hierarchies.

Through our conferences, online ministry tracks and workshops, webinars, catechetical journal, local events, Guild small group circles and discussion forums, personal mentorship, and wealth of resources, we seek to support all those involved in the care of souls to grow in pastoral gentleness, faithful creativity, and bold confidence as they reach out to evangelize, accompany, and pass on the Catholic faith to others in the power of the Holy Spirit.

www.ingramcontent.com/pod-product-compliance
Lightning Source LLC
LaVergne TN
LVHW051516070426
835507LV00023B/3144